GREEK MYTHOLOGY

HERACLES

Stephanides Brothers'

GREEK MYTHOLOGY

HERACLES

C_&

Retold by Menelaos Stephanides
Drawings by Yannis Stephanides

Translation
Bruce Walter

SIGMA

HERACLES

Published worldwide by Sigma Publications
This edition published in 2022

SIGMA PUBLICATIONS
42, Tebon Street, Ag. Dimitrios, 173 43 Athens, Greece
Tel.: +30 210 3607667, Fax: +30 210 3638941
www.sigmapublications.com
e-mail:sigma@sigmapublications.com

ISBN: 978-960-425-065-3

HEROES: men mighty, unflinching and fair in spirit, mind and body. They may not have been quite as men envisaged them in those distant, mythical years, yet they did exist. For there have always been heroes and always will be. As long as there is cowardice, there will be daring, as long as there is evil, there will be virtue, too; as long as there is meanness of spirit, there will be generosity. For the bad gives birth to the good as the winter brings the spring. The common man loves a hero. He places his trust in him and draws strength from his example – that strength which has enabled mankind to forge onwards and upwards.

TABLE OF CONTENTS

A HERO IS BORN

The story of Heracles' birth

In those distant days when men believed that mighty Zeus ruled over gods and men there lived on this earth, in the land of Greece, a hero whom men admired and loved above the gods themselves. His name was Heracles and in daring and in number his feats outshone any the world had ever seen before.

Heracles was such a towering figure that no single region could hold him within its narrow boundaries. He became the hero of all Greece and something beyond that still: the heroic expression of the hopes and yearnings of all the Hellenes.

At that time, as everybody knows, Greece was divided into many small city-states forever making war on one another – and the result was ruin and despair. Yet everyone spoke the same language, worshipped the same gods and shared the same love of life and peace. And so, little by little, it became the longing of all the peoples of Greece to be united into one state.

But it remained a mere wish.

It is this wish that the language of mythology expresses so beautifully in the story of the birth of Heracles.

In those days men believed that all great issues were settled by the gods of Olympus. Zeus himself, they felt, wanted the Greek states to be united and so he decided to father a son, Heracles, who would grow up to be a hero mighty enough to accomplish this desire.

The city which this son of Zeus was to rule would be none other than golden Mycenae, the proudest, richest and most powerful city in all the land.

Mycenae had been founded by the great hero Perseus, himself a son of Zeus. On the death of Perseus, his son Electryon came to the throne. Electryon had nine sons and a daughter, Alcmene, who would one day become the mother of Heracles.

Tall and stately, Alcmene was the fairest and wisest woman in the world. Thick, silky tresses framed her lovely face and long dark lashes set off her large and expressive eyes. Electryon's daughter had all the natural graces that became a woman destined to be the mother of heroes. And if Zeus fathered the child, she would certainly give birth to the greatest hero who had ever appeared on the face of this earth. This is why, of all women, mortal and immortal, he chose Alcmene to be the mother of Heracles.

Of course, Zeus was already married to Hera; but either because men liked to believe that heroes and great leaders should have some god for a father, or because certain kings liked to boast that they were the sons of Zeus, the ancient Greeks considered it no shame to say that the gods fathered children on any woman they pleased. Whatever the case may be, it is said that after the birth of Heracles no other woman ever bore a child by Zeus again.

As he had done on previous occasions, Zeus employed cunning to achieve his aim. And he had to wait quite a while before the opportunity presented itself.

But let us begin the story from the beginning.

Alcmene's father, Electryon, had promised his daughter in marriage to Amphitryon, king of Troezen. But tragedy struck Mycenae and the wedding was postponed. All Alcmene's brothers were killed in battle with the fearsome Teleboans, a race of men with ear-shattering voices who had seized Electryon's herds and wished to place their own king on the throne of Mycenae. Failing to achieve this goal, they had to give the cattle to Polyxenus, king of the Elids, so he could hide them away. However, Amphitryon found them and, wishing to help his future father-in-law, he purchased the animals and brought them to Mycenae.

To his surprise, Electryon was furious.

"What right does Polyxenus have to sell off stolen animals – and how could you agree to such a shameful bargain?" he cried in anger.

"By all the gods!" exclaimed Amphitryon. "I was only trying to help you! I would rather see your herds in the darkest depths of Hades than have men killed on their account!" And in exasperation he flung his heavy club into the midst of the herd. It was only a moment of fury but the result was a tragedy which could never be undone. For the club hit the horns of a bull, rebounded, struck Electryon on the head and laid him in the dust, dead.

After this misfortune Electryon was succeeded on the throne of Mycenae by his brother Sthenelus while Amphitryon, grief stricken by the harm he had unwittingly caused, gave up everything he possessed including the kingdom of Troezen (which was taken by Sthenelus) and left for Thebes, where Creon ruled.

Yet not for a moment did he cease to love Alcmene, and in the end he sent a man to Mycenae to beg her forgiveness for the evil he had accidentally done her, and to ask whether she still wished to marry him in spite of everything.

It was then that Zeus planted in Alcmene's mind the answer which would serve his purpose.

"I agree to marry Amphitryon," Alcmene told the messenger, "but only on condition that immediately the wedding rites have been celebrated he will make war on the Teleboans and take revenge for the death of all my brothers. This is not my wish alone; I believe it to be my dead father's, too."

Amphitryon was willing to do anything to win Alcmene and he certainly did not flinch at this demand. But with whose army? For he no longer had troops of his own. He immediately applied to Creon, king of Thebes, but was told:

"I will give you the army that you want, but only if you rid Thebes of the Teumessian vixen."

Now the Teumessian vixen was a fearsome, bloodthirsty beast which had wrought havoc in the neighbourhood of Thebes. To keep her savagery within bounds, the Thebans were obliged every month to give her a male child to devour, as the oracle had decreed. This was a terrible sacrifice to make, and yet it seemed impossible to kill the vixen, for it was written that neither man nor beast would ever be able to match her speed and bring her down. And as if this were not enough, the vixen was under the protection of the sea god, Poseidon.

Amphitryon was almost in despair when he was helped by Cephalus king of Athens who gave him Laelaps, a dog with god-given powers which could never lose its prey.

"But bring him back as soon as you can," the king asked. "Laelaps is a sacred animal. He was once a gift from Zeus to Europa, daughter of Agenor."

Amphitryon took the dog and set off in pursuit of the Teumessian vixen. Laelaps soon picked up the scent and began to hunt her down.

So the fox that could never be caught and the dog who could never lose its prey set off on a wild chase. But which of the two would win? This was a problem not only for Amphitryon and the Thebans but for the gods themselves, who assembled to consider the matter.

For if Laelaps caught the vixen, of what value were the words written by the Fates? Not to mention that they all feared the wrath of her protector, Poseidon. On the other hand, if she did escape, what would the gift the gods had bestowed on Laelaps be worth? And again, would any of them dare resist the will of Zeus, who was certain to demand victory for Laelaps? In the end it was Zeus himself who found the solution; one that pleased him and was acceptable to the other gods as well. He transformed both Laelaps and the Teumessian vixen into lifeless stone images.

This meant, of course, that Amphitryon was unable to return the sacred dog to Cephalus; but he more than made it up to him by the gift of one of the islands he later took from the Teleboans. The island is now known as Cephalonia, and it took its name from its new king, Cephalus.

But most important of all, Thebes was relieved of its sacrifice of blood and Amphitryon obtained the army which he needed – not just any army but a band of soldiers eager to serve and lay down their lives for the saviour of the children of Thebes. Now Amphitryon could keep the promise Alcmene had demanded of him.

And so the wedding at last took place – but only the wedding. For as soon as the ceremony was

*... So the fox that could never be caught
and the dog who could never lose its prey
set off on a wild chase ...*

over, Amphitryon bade farewell to his bride and set off at the head of his army to do battle against the Teleboans.

Alcmene went back to the palace, locked herself in her room alone and waited for the return of her husband – the husband she herself had sent to war though she loved him with all her heart.

All these things happened by the will of mighty Zeus, ruler of gods and men. His plans were now laid.

After Alcmene had been sitting alone for a few days, Zeus transformed himself into the shape of Amphitryon, opened the door of the young bride's room and rushed in crying enthusiastically: "Victory! A brilliant victory! We have crushed the Teleboans!" And with a face wreathed in joy he swept her into his arms and kissed her. Then he told Alcmene the whole story of the battle he had supposedly fought, even giving her vivid accounts of his own feats of valour!

These details added the final touch to his disguise. Convinced that this man was her husband, Alcmene took Zeus into her arms without the least suspicion and spent a long night of bliss with him.

For this was no ordinary night, but one which

lasted three whole nights together. Such was the will of mighty Zeus.

To achieve this he had summoned Hermes and commanded him to fly to the sun god, Helios, with the message that by Zeus' order he remain in his shining palace all day without making his customary journey across the heavens.

As soon as that was done, Zeus sent Hermes to the Hours with instructions not to make ready Helios' winged horses and gleaming chariot, so that even if he did not wish to, the god of day would be obliged to obey his sovereign.

So, willy-nilly, Helios missed his daily course across the face of the earth and remained at home in his palace, muttering: "What a state of affairs! Things were better when great Cronus ruled. Then, at least, we knew the difference between day and night – and he didn't leave his wife to go running off having adventures in Thebes!"

But Zeus had not yet finished with Hermes, and so the messenger of the gods went next to Selene, the moon, and commanded her to prolong her stay in the sky that night. And the moon, like her brother the sun, had no choice but to obey.

Finally, Hermes went to Hypnos, the god of sleep, and told him that by Zeus' decree he should sink all mankind into a heavy slumber that night. This order, too, was carried out; and thus not a soul on earth suspected that one night's sleep had lasted the length of three.

Finally, however, the late dawn broke, Zeus disappeared, and a little later the real Amphitryon appeared upon the scene.

Bursting with enthusiasm, for he had returned victorious, he rushed to embrace his bride. But she, naturally enough, showed no great joy at seeing him.

"But aren't you glad to see me?" Amphitryon demanded in astonishment.

"Why should I be?" Alcmene replied. "We've been together all night, haven't we?"

Amphitryon was baffled by this reply, but so excited was he by his victory and their reunion that he gave it no special thought. Instead, he launched into a detailed description of the great battle and his heroic part in it.

"Stirring deeds, I grant you, husband," Alcmene

responded, "but I see no particular reason why I should have to listen to them twice!"

Amphitryon could not believe his ears. He said nothing to Alcmene, however, but went instead to the oracle at Delphi to seek some explanation for her bewildering remarks.

There he learned of all that had happened in his absence, and was also told that in due course his wife would give birth to two sons, one of whom would be the child of Zeus and was destined to become the mightiest hero in the whole of Greece.

Nine months went by, until, one evening, as the gods sat eating and drinking in the shining halls of Olympus, Zeus rose from the table and announced:

"Immortals, hear my words. My joy at this hour is so great I can no longer keep my secret to myself. The first child born tonight of the line of Perseus will be my son. He will grow into the greatest hero ever seen upon the face of this earth and all the peoples of Greece will bow to his will. Heracles shall be his name."

When she heard these words, Hera was consumed with jealousy. Yet again her husband had fathered a child on another woman! Unable to contain herself, she whispered something into the ear of the cunning goddess Ate who was seated at her side, then she turned to Zeus and snapped:

"As usual, you promise great things in your cups, but by morning you have forgotten, and nothing ever comes of it. This time, I want you to swear a solemn oath before us all that the first child born this night of the line of Perseus will indeed be the great hero you have told us of and that all the peoples of Greece will bow to his will."

Without a moment's thought, the unsuspecting Zeus gave an oath which could never be broken.

"Yes," he cried, "I swear by the sacred waters of the Styx that it shall be as I say!"

When Hera heard her husband's vow, she smiled knowingly to herself. For, at Mycenae, Nicippe the wife of Sthenelus was awaiting a child; and Sthenelus, like Alcmene's father, was a son of Perseus. Granted, Nicippe was only seven months gone, but this was no problem for Hera. She immediately ordered Eileithyia, goddess of child-birth, to hasten to Thebes, prolong Alcmene's labour pains, and then go straight on to Mycenae and bring Nicippe's child into the world before its time.

Hera's commands were carried out to the letter, and so, for all Zeus' well-laid plans, the first child born that night of the line of Perseus was Eurystheus of Mycenae, a sickly, timid creature dragged into the world two months before he was due. An hour afterwards Heracles was born, immediately followed by another boy, Iphicles, who had been fathered by Amphitryon.

Shortly after the birth of Heracles, Hera appeared before Zeus.

"I fear I must disappoint you!" she sneered. "The first child born tonight of Perseus' line was not your son but Eurystheus, son of Sthenelus, king of Mycenae. And by the oath you swore it will be Eurystheus who commands, and Heracles who shall obey!"

Zeus was speechless with fury. All his wonderful plans had suddenly gone awry. This was terrible, unbelievable – and yet it was true. "Eurystheus will command and Heracles shall obey." Zeus himself had sworn it by the sacred waters of the Styx.

Thus Hera deceived the great ruler of gods and men, and the dream of generations would remain a dream. For Eurystheus, of course, was utterly incapable of becoming the true leader of all Greece.

Zeus' rage was frightening to behold. He could not begin to imagine how he could have fallen into such a trap. As soon as he set eyes on Ate he understood everything. It was she who had clouded his judgement and caught him unawares – but she would pay for it! Seizing the goddess by her braided hair, he flung her from Olympus with superhuman force. Ever since that day, cunning Ate has lived on earth below, among men and women. And every underhand deed committed by mortals is ascribed to her scheming influence. Even the Greek word for fraud means "that which comes from Ate."

When Zeus had thrown Ate out of Olympus, he turned to the other gods and said:

"Alas, I gave a sacred vow and cannot take back my words. Heracles will not become the great leader Greece has so long stood in need of. Instead, he will suffer such pain and hardship that it grieves me to think of it. But he will also accomplish twelve great labours and many other marvellous feats, and he will be praised and admired as neither god nor man has ever been praised before. And when his life on earth comes to an end, he will be received on Olympus. He will become immortal, and Hera herself will accept him as her equal and her friend."

But Hera, hearing all this, only said to herself:

"What a fool Zeus is to think that I shall ever be reconciled with Alcmene's brat! Oh, no! That will never be, for the simple reason that Heracles will not live. I shall see to it that he dies while he is still a baby – now, while it's easy."

But instead of that, Hera accomplished something which did not please her at all.

One evening, Zeus planted a fear in Alcmene's mind that his wife would do some harm to the infant Heracles that very night. To protect her child from Hera's wrath, Alcmene took young Heracles from the palace and left him in a lonely spot beneath the walls of Thebes, calling on the goddess Athena to protect her little boy.

Acting on Zeus' orders, Athena took Hera out walking in the neighbourhood of Thebes and, making it look like mere coincidence, brought her to the very place where Heracles was lying.

When Hera saw the child, she cried out in surprise:

"A baby alone in the wilderness! And what a little darling he is! I never saw such a lovely, healthy child!"

Athena gave Hera a sidelong glance and added:

"Who knows how many hours it's been lying here abandoned. There is so much heartlessness in this world! You have milk, my lady. Why not give him a little? He must be very thirsty!"

Hera willingly gave the baby her breast, but Heracles sucked with such strength and hurt her so much that she pushed him violently from her and the milk spurted from her nipple up into the dark heavens. And that is how the galaxy was created. But that was not the only result. When Heracles drank Hera's milk he became immortal. Instead of destroying him as she had planned, the goddess had made him indestructible.

The angry Hera was about to hurry Athena away when footsteps were heard.

"Let us hide," suggested Athena, "and see who is

... Hera willingly gave the baby her breast ...

coming."

When they saw it was Alcmene, hurrying to fetch
her child, Hera bit her lip, pale with fury. For now
she saw the meaning of what had happened. Just
as she had tricked Zeus so now her turn had come.
She knew there was nothing she could say, but she
looked at Alcmene, lovelier than a goddess in the
moonlight, and her jealousy was redoubled – and
with it her determination to destroy Heracles. If she
could bestow immortality, then it must be within her
power to take it away again.

From then on Zeus entrusted Athena with the
task of protecting young Heracles and the goddess
of wisdom did everything in her power to help the
child. She sent her owl, the bird of wisdom, to keep
sentinel over his cradle and thus the boy, too, ac-
quired wisdom, not only by the day but by the hour,
guarded by the watchful bird, which kept him safe
from every danger and fanned him with its wings
through the hot summer nights.

Alcmene rocked the twins to sleep in a great hanging shield, which made a wonderful cradle. This
shield had once belonged to the king of the Teleboans,

and was part of the booty Amphitryon had brought back from the battle. The two brothers often played inside it as it swung in the air, but Heracles was such a lively baby that one day he pushed Iphicles right over the rim. Alcmene heard his cries when he hit the floor below and came running to see what had happened. Fortunately, Iphicles was not hurt; though to put her mind at rest the queen immediately had the shield lowered to the ground.

But the true measure of the strength in young Heracles' tiny body was not revealed until Hera made her first attempt to kill him.

Her opportunity came one night when the owl left its post to find and punish a spider which had ruined Athena's finest piece of embroidery. Before leaving, of course, the owl warned Alcmene to guard her children, and she set twelve strapping serving girls to keep watch over them till the owl's return.

The servants sat doing their needlework in the children's room, but when the hour came to put out the lamps their eyelids grew heavy and one after the other their heads sank upon their breasts and sleep overcame them.

The last of the girls had scarcely nodded off when through the half open door slithered two huge snakes sent by Hera on their murderous mission. The moonlight shone through the window onto the babies and the two snakes made straight for their cradle.

But even the tiny noise they made as they slid across the floor was enough to wake young Heracles. He spotted them immediately and sprang upright in the cradle, ready to face the danger which threatened. His sudden movement awakened Iphicles, who shrieked with terror when he set eyes on the snakes. His cries awoke the servants; when they saw the two huge serpents in the room they were so frightened that they rushed out, screaming for help. Alcmene heard their cries and aroused Amphitryon. The guards sprang into wakefulness and the whole palace was soon astir. Sword in hand, and followed by his wife, Amphitryon charged into the children's room with a band of soldiers at their heels. The scene that met their eyes was beyond belief! Heracles sat there clutching two huge snakes, which twitched and shuddered in his vice-like grip. Amphitryon raised his sword to kill them, but saw there was no longer

... Heracles sat there clutching two huge snakes,
which twitched and shuddered in his vice-like grip ...

any need. Heracles threw their lifeless bodies at the feet of his astounded step-father while Iphicles, not surprisingly, continued to whimper with fear.

So Hera's murderous attempt came to nothing, while all who witnessed the scene realized that this child was destined to perform great deeds. And Amphitryon, who till this moment had not known which of the two boys was his own, now stood in awe before the son of Zeus.

Heracles grows to manhood

From then on, Amphitryon took even more care of Heracles than of his own child. To teach him, he appointed the greatest sages, the most famous artists and the most outstanding gymnasts of the times. Heracles learned to read and write, was taught literature, philosophy and astronomy and was trained in music and song. But above all he was coached in gymnastics and exercised in every branch of athletics, as well as in the arts of war.

Amphitryon himself taught the boy the skills of charioteering. From an early age, too, he was trained to shoot an arrow with unerring aim, to throw a lance further than anyone, to handle a sword with dazzling dexterity and to wield the heaviest of clubs as if it were a mere twig. Heracles also became a matchless wrestler, a formidable boxer and the fleetest of runners. And besides all these he mastered the most cunning strategies of war.

Heracles never used his strength to do wanton harm to others, but on the other hand he would submit to ill-treatment or abuse from no one. Whoever provoked his terrible wrath would bring dire consequences on himself, and this is what befell Linus, who taught the young man music.

Heracles loved music as much as all his other lessons, but when it came to learning the lyre, he ran into serious difficulties. His fingers were so thick and strong that he was forever breaking the strings, and his teacher Linus would get so exasperated that he cursed gods and demons alike. Heracles tried his hardest, but he could do no better, and once, when he was doing a difficult exercise, he broke all the strings together. Linus lost all patience and began to beat his pupil so furiously you would have thought he was trying to kill him. Sick of lesson and teacher alike, Heracles flung the lyre at Linus' head; but he was unable to control his strength, and the instrument struck Linus with such force that he fell to the ground, dead.

Next day, young Heracles was brought before the courts.

"You have killed your teacher," the judges told him. "You are guilty of a terrible crime."

"Truly, I had no wish to kill him," Heracles replied. "I am deeply sorry for what happened."

"There can be no excuse for such an act," came the judges' stern answer.

But Heracles was able to defend himself. All the wise teaching he had received had not been in vain.

"I told you it was not my wish to kill him; and there is an excuse. You are judges, and you must know the law lays down that he who is attacked has the right to retaliate. This was decreed by Rhadamanthys, son of Zeus and Europa, and the greatest law-maker in all Greece."

The judges were at a loss for words when they heard this. They conferred together and finally brought in their verdict: Heracles was innocent.

But Amphitryon feared that his step-son's strength might cause him to commit other acts of violence; and so he sent him to watch over his herds in their pastures on Mount Cithaeron.

Heracles stayed up on the mountain for two years. There, he turned from boy into man, his muscles hardened and his strength grew even greater.

The mountain was also grazed by the herds of king Thespius, who ruled over the neighbouring city which bore his name. On his visits to Cithaeron Thespius often met Heracles, and the two men became friends.

One day, the king came running in alarm. A fearsome lion had fallen upon his herds and wrought bloody havoc among them. Soon some villagers arrived on the scene, followed by other herdsmen. Fear and anxiety were written on every face. But there was one man who was not afraid. This was young Heracles – and it did not take him long to reach a decision.

Without saying a word to anyone, he disappeared into the forest where he first cut a great club from a wild olive tree and then went in search of the lion's spoor. Finding the beast's footprints, he followed them to the spring where it came for water. Hiding behind a rock, he lay in wait, and when the lion appeared he sprang on it with his club and gave it such a blow that a second was not needed. The powerful beast sank lifeless at the young hero's feet.

When the news spread of the lion's death, words of praise for the bold young man were heard on every hand. All spoke of his determination, strength and daring. The admiring Thespius invited Heracles to his palace where his daughters –he was said to have fifty– offered him their hospitality for fifty days and … nights.

With Virtue and Evil

In the meantime, Thebes had fallen on evil days. Erginus, king of nearby Orchomenus, had launched a massive attack on the city, defeated Creon, and imposed a heavy annual tribute on the Thebans. Convinced that only Heracles might save the day, Amphitryon ordered the young man to return.

Leaving his cattle in the care of the other herds-men, Heracles set off for Thebes.

On the way, he suddenly came face to face with two women. They were both very beautiful, but otherwise quite unlike in appearance.

One of them was even lovelier than the other – or at least she seemed to be at first sight. She was so well-groomed, her hair so fashionably dressed and her face so artfully made up that in her gorgeous robe and gleaming jewels she looked ravishingly beautiful. Add to this her bewitching smile, her beckoning eyes, the graceful sway of her body and her heady perfume and it is not hard to see why she drew all men's eyes upon her.

"My name is Joy," she liked to say, but it was rumoured that her real name was Evil.

The other woman was simple and unaffected, but with a natural beauty that could not pass unnoticed. Not that she was indifferent to the way she looked, by any means; but the care she took over her appear-ance showed an instinctive respect both for herself and others. In her eyes and in her movements there was an inborn feminine grace, while her finely chiselled features reflected the nobility of her spirit. Her name was Virtue. Unadorned, serious and utterly lovely, she was a true goddess.

When Heracles saw the two women he was impressed, but baffled.

"How different these two are – and what can they want from me?" he wondered. He did not have to wonder for long.

"We have been sent by the gods to help you choose your road in life," Virtue told him.

"And the choice is not hard to make," added the first woman, taking him by the hand with a flirtatious smile. "Look at me and you will see what pleasures life has to offer you. You are strong and handsome, and if you so desire, the road before you can be filled with comfort and delights, for many will seek your company and friendship. Come with me, and I will show you how to savour each hour of every day. Life is short, but it has much to offer the man who does not squander his time in thankless tasks which only others profit from. Enjoy good company, my friend; taste of the choicest foods and drink the finest wines; sleep carefree and let others be plagued

*... Look at me and you will see
what pleasures life has to offer you ...*

by the troubles of this world, since that is what they were born for. You were made for pleasure, and that's so easy to see that I need say no more."

"Truly, how wonderful life will be if I only do as she tells me," thought Heracles, and he turned on his heel to follow the first woman without even waiting to hear the second.

But as he was doing so, he heard her voice behind him.

"Where are you going, Heracles, son of Zeus?" Her commanding air, the sternness of her tone and her compelling gaze showed that he had acted neither wisely nor well.

"The mighty and the bold," continued Virtue, "have finer things by far to do than spend their time in idle pleasures. I cannot promise you an easy road, but it shall be a fair one. That which is good and noble is always difficult and calls for strength of will and courage; and these you have, Heracles."

"Do not listen to her," the first woman broke in. "She wants to rob you of all the joys of life!"

"Then let him go with you and enjoy the delights you hold out to him," retorted Virtue. "Off you go, young man; enjoy life's pleasures to the end – if you can. For some day your friends will tire of you, all doors will be locked in your face; and then you will realize that you have done nothing, made nothing of yourself and given nothing to others, in spite of the gifts you were born with. For you are strong in soul and body as no man has ever been before. And for the strong and the brave, the road that lies ahead is a splendid one but hard: the road of the hero who rejoices when he helps mankind and defeats the powers of evil and injustice. For victory in the face of daunting odds brings true joy, while the fruit of earthly pleasures is mere bitterness. Forge onwards, Heracles! Oppose the evil, support the weak, rid the world of monsters, labour for mankind without regard for the weariness and even humiliation it may cost you. This is all I have to say to you. Follow me if you will."

"Goddess, I thank you for your help," replied Heracles, his mind made up. "I shall follow the road you have shown me."

The moment he uttered these words, the two women disappeared.

Now Heracles knew what he must do, and with quickened step he made his way towards Thebes.

The war with Orchomenus

A little further on he reached a crossroads; and there he halted at the sight of a troop of soldiers approaching. They did not seem to be Thebans. Heracles waited for them, and when they came close he called out in a commanding voice:

"Who are you, and where are you going?"

"Since when need we explain ourselves to Thebans?" their leader retorted.

"This is Theban land you stand on," replied an angry Heracles, drawing his bow, "and if you wish to pass, it will be over my dead body."

"Get him!" barked the foreign captain in fury, hurling his lance at the hero.

Quick as a flash, Heracles dodged behind a tree, and the lance sank quivering into its trunk. Tensing his bowstring, Heracles shot an arrow – and did not miss his mark. The battle grew fierce, but it was brief. All the intruders were wounded, as Heracles had intended, and in the end they fell on their knees and begged his mercy.

"Tell me first who you are," the hero commanded, "and why you have come into our land!"

"We are from Orchomenus," the wounded men replied. "We were sent here by our king, Erginus, to levy the tribute promised us by Creon."

Then Heracles bound them, single file, with their hands trussed behind their backs, and told them:

"Go back to your king. Show him your wounds and your bonds and tell him that from now on the Thebans will pay their tribute in such coin and worse!"

Roped together and humiliated, the soldiers made their way back to Orchomenus while Heracles continued on the road to Thebes, his spirits lifted.

When he reached the city, however, he found the situation was bad. Amphitryon's face was lined with worry, while Iphicles stood by raging helplessly.

"Listen, Heracles," Amphitryon told him. "The city of Cadmus has been defeated and put to shame. Seven-gated Thebes has bent the knee before Orchomenus, a lesser city in every way. Our people are burdened with a heavy tribute and sunk in poverty and grief. At any moment now we are expecting the soldiers of Erginus to come and demand their due."

"Share the tribute out again amongst the people," replied Heracles, "and prepare for war against Erginus."

And he told them of all that had happened on the road to Thebes.

"But what shall we fight with?" Iphicles demanded. "When Erginus defeated us he carried off all our weapons and horses, and forbade us to rearm. Besides, only one thing concerns Creon, and that is keeping his throne."

"We can arm ourselves, and we must do so at once," Heracles answered. "As I was coming here I stepped into a temple and I found it filled with weapons dedicated to the gods."

"Yes," replied Amphitryon, "there are such arms in all the temples. But they are the weapons and armour of the dead, or booty captured in former Theban victories. I do not know if it is right to take them. Perhaps the gods will turn against us if we do."

"The gods will say that we are worthy of our fate

if we sit here empty-handed while our enemies approach."

"Heracles is right, father," Iphicles broke in. "The gods will not help those who do not arm themselves."

"You are both right," Amphitryon decided. "Let us go and arouse the Thebans."

Within a few days the whole city had been alerted. Heracles and Iphicles collected all the young men, and together they went into the temples, took the weapons and distributed them. There were bows, swords, lances, shields, helmets and even whole suits of armour. Although a few people muttered that this was sacrilege, the goddess Athena encouraged Heracles to carry on, regardless of protest.

Military training was begun immediately. Every day, Heracles drilled the young men in the handling of their weapons; and although Creon was still afraid that someone might make a bid for his throne, he knew he had nothing to fear from this quarter. He was well aware that royal titles were the last thing the bold young hero coveted. And so he was only too willing to make Heracles commander of the new army of Thebes.

When Erginus and his troops reached the city, they were surprised to find forces opposing them. But at the sight of the pitiful assortment of old weapons the Thebans were armed with, they fell upon them laughing, confident of an easy victory.

It was no victory, however, but a defeat. Erginus himself was killed by Heracles, and the Thebans pursued his army back to the very walls of Orchomenus. But the war did not end with this battle, for the enemy still had powerful reserves within the city and

formidable charioteers, while all the Theban horses had been carried off by Erginus.

Heracles was the one who found a way around this problem. Thebes was separated from Orchomenus by a broad plain watered by the river Cephissus. This river did not flow directly into the sea, but disappeared underground through huge sinkholes, passing beneath a mountainous region before its waters reached the coast. By shifting huge masses of earth, Heracles blocked the subterranean exits of the river, which flooded the whole plain to form the broad lake of Copais.

The enemy could not cross this watery barrier, and so they were obliged to fight the next battle in the mountainous region, where their chariots could not be used. The result was another victory for the Thebans; but nothing is won without sacrifice, and this time the whole of Thebes mourned Amphitryon, who had died a hero's death in the fighting. However, the city had regained its independence and was not only freed of its obligation to pay tribute but made Orchomenus pay back double the amount.

In his gratitude, Creon gave Heracles his daughter Megara in marriage, and half his palace; while to Iphicles he gave his younger daughter.

All the gods of Olympus came to the wedding of Heracles and Megara, except Hera of course, and they brought rich gifts with them.

These gifts of the gods were a tribute to the hero's prowess. Zeus gave him a shield stronger than any ever made before; Athena's gift was a golden breast-plate, while Hephaestus presented him with a helmet encrusted with diamonds. Apollo gave a golden bow and a quiver full of arrows, Hermes a keen-edged sword and Poseidon two horses as swift as the storm winds of the sea.

The madness of Heracles

Megara bore Heracles three children and the couple were happy. But the hero's happiness and his ever more glorious victories filled Hera with bitter resentment and she resolved to harm him once again.

And so, one day, while Heracles was contentedly watching his children at play, Ate the goddess of fraud crept up silently behind him. She threw an invisible veil over his eyes with the magic power to rob him of his reason. Immediately, the hero's vision was clouded, and in place of his children he saw three fearsome dragons rearing to strike. Seizing chairs, tables and whatever else lay within reach, he broke them over what he thought were the dragons' heads – thus, alas, killing his own children. Then, seized with demonic rage, he smashed and ruined everything in the palace, while everyone inside scrambled for the doors or hurled themselves through the windows to escape the wild rampage of the strongest man the world had ever seen.

When Creon's palace was no more than a heap of stones, Ate returned and removed the invisible veil which had covered his eyes. And then the unhappy father saw, amid the wreckage, not dragons but his own three children lying slain. His eyes could not believe the terrible truth they told him. How could he have slaughtered his darling children with his own hands? Even the thought of it was too horrible to contemplate.

After this hideous deed, Creon ordered Heracles to leave Thebes instantly, and his wife let it be known that she never wished to set eyes on him again. But there was no need for them to tell him; Heracles took the path of exile of his own accord, and his wanderings eventually brought him to the land of Thespia.

There, in a voice hoarse with anguish, he told his friend king Thespius of the vile crime he had committed, and then, for all his strength and courage, he broke down and cried like a child begging for help.

Thespius took pity on Heracles and received him as a guest, doing everything in his power to try and make the hero forget. But it was all in vain; nothing could wipe that dreadful scene from his memory.

And so the days went by until, eventually, messengers came to Thespius from Mycenae bringing news that king Sthenelus had died and that his son Eurystheus now ruled in his stead. They also said that they bore a message for Heracles from their new king. The hero had been sitting nearby, silent and lost in sad thoughts, but when he heard his name he rose, took the letter in his hands and read its contents.

"I, the great king of Mycenae," the letter ran, "whom Zeus himself has given right of command over all the peoples of Greece, now order Heracles, son of Amphitryon, to enter my service to accomplish twelve great labours which shall bring glory on my name and on my kingdom. Thus I, Eurystheus, son of Sthenelus and descendant of Zeus through the hero Perseus, have decreed."

When Heracles had read this summons he was in two minds as to what to do. Thespius, who saw the ridiculous presumption of Eurystheus' demand, advised him not to go. But the gods were not of the same opinion. Great Zeus was bound by the vow he had sworn all those years ago and could do nothing. Now Hera had the word, and her hatred of Alcmene's son was deadly. By setting a pitiful little braggart like Eurystheus to order Heracles about, she could not only humiliate the hero but bring about his downfall.

The dangers he might face were of no account to Heracles, however, and as for humiliation it was the very thing he sought, for he wished to wash away the stain of his crime against his children.

The only thing that made him hesitate was the thought of serving such an unworthy and despicable man. Might it not do the human race more harm than good? In his confusion he decided to consult the oracle at Delphi to learn what he must do. The reply was as follows:

"Go to Mycenae and enter the service of Eurystheus. He will command you to carry out twelve great labours. Only when you have completed the last of them will the gods forgive you for your crime against your children."

Heracles was filled with relief when he heard the oracle's words. At last he knew the path that he must follow.

THE TWELVE LABOURS

In the service of Eurystheus

Heracles set off for Mycenae without delay, accompanied on his journey by Iolaus, the brave young son of Iphicles.

When they reached Mycenae, he went alone to the palace and asked to see king Eurystheus.

The guards told him to wait at the entrance, for they had strict orders not to allow him inside.

Eurystheus came to the palace gate to see what manner of man this was who would bring glory on his name and on his kingdom.

But the moment he saw the hero's hulking frame and grim features he let out a frightened squeal and scuttled back to the palace to hide.

For this "great king of Mycenae" was but half the height of Heracles, ugly, skinny, pasty-faced and such a coward he was afraid of his own shadow.

"Run! Run! Close the gates! Don't let Heracles
in!" he shouted. "Woe betide you if any harm befalls
me!"

Locking himself in his room he curled up in a
frightened ball upon the bed and lay huddled there
wondering how he could rid himself of Heracles.
Finally he decided that the only way to avoid another
shock like this was to set the hero a task of such
difficulty that he would never survive to darken his
palace gates again. He racked his brains for hours,
but only succeeded in making himself so tired and
despondent that he fell into an exhausted sleep. And
while he slept, the god of dreams came at Hera's
command and put a vision into his mind which
helped him to decide where Heracles should be sent.

The first labour: The Nemean lion

In those days, there lived in the forests of Nemea
a huge and terrifying lion. It had the strength of ten
ordinary lions and its hide was so tough that neither
arrow, lance nor the keenest sword could pierce it. It

... he let out a frightened squeal and scuttled
back to the palace to hide ...

was the offspring of Typhoon, the monster who had wrestled with Zeus himself, and the equally fearsome Echidna, half woman and half snake. Its brothers and sisters were the Lernaean Hydra, Cerberus, Chimaera, the Sphinx and other hideous monsters whom the gods themselves were afraid to face in combat.

When Eurystheus saw this monstrous lion in his dream, he let out such a shriek that the whole palace came running to see what else had befallen their "great" king.

But as soon as Eurystheus realized he had only been dreaming, he took courage and a crafty smile stole across his features. Now he knew just where to send Heracles so he might never set eyes on him again.

In a cracked and petulant voice he immediately called, not for Heracles, of course, but for Copreus, his herald. He called and called again, sounding more like an old shrew than a king, and when the herald was finally found and appeared before him he was ordered to go straight to Heracles and convey the command of the "mighty king of Mycenae": to hunt down and kill the Nemean lion.

Copreus, whose name means "dung" in Greek, by the way, could hardly wait to deliver his master's wishes. It was no small honour to give orders to such a hero.

When Heracles heard this he had no suspicion of the kind of lion he had been pitted against, and imagined he would be able to kill it easily. So, taking up the club he had used against the lion of Cithaeron, he slung his bow and quiver over his shoulder and set off for Nemea.

On his way, he met a poor man named Molorchus who was standing outside his hut preparing to offer a sacrifice to the gods. After greeting him, Heracles asked who the sacrifice was in honour of, and he received this reply:

"In honour of our guardian, Zeus. I wish to thank him for keeping the Nemean lion away from my door."

"Do not make your sacrifice yet awhile," Heracles replied, "for I have been ordered by Eurystheus to find the beast and despatch it. I have killed lions before, and I am not afraid. Yet lest anything should happen to me, if I do not return within thirty days then offer your sacrifice in memory of the soul of Heracles, son of Alcmene. But if I return, as I believe I shall, then we shall celebrate together in honour of almighty Zeus."

"Heracles, son of Alcmene," the poor man cried, "it is a pity to throw away your life in vain! You cannot know what kind of lion you have been sent to fight. If this creature had been spawned by a lion, it might not be beyond your powers to kill it. But it was not. It comes from a line of monsters – and what monsters! It was fathered by Typhoon and Echidna gave it birth. There is no killing this beast – and even if you had all the gods of Olympus at your side you would not return alive. For years, now, we have gone in fear of it. Our flocks have been decimated, the countryside laid waste, and none of those with courage enough to hunt the monster down has ever lived to tell the tale."

Now Heracles realized why Eurystheus had sent him to carry out such a task. But his determination was not shaken, and in a resolute voice he said, "I will go to find this lion; for I must either kill it or die in the attempt. Farewell – and if we do not meet again, do as I told you." And with these words he struck out for the mountains.

Molorchus admired the hero's stubborn courage, but as he watched him go he wished with all his heart he had been able to make him stay.

As he walked along, Heracles looked around until he spotted a wild olive with a thick and knotted trunk as hard as iron. He tore it from the ground, roots and all, and from it fashioned a new and formidable club which was even more massive than his old one. Tossing that aside, he shouldered his new weapon and continued on his way. Later it occurred to him that he might need to lie in wait for the lion for days and nights on end, and that he would need all the strength he possessed to last out. So he found a quiet spot, lay down and fell into a deep sleep. Ten days and nights they say Heracles slept, and he awoke with all his powers renewed. When he rose, he washed in a spring and set off refreshed and filled with hope in search of the lion. After wandering for many days in a landscape empty of all living creatures, he eventually found the lion's spoor. The huge padmarks were sunk deep into the ground, showing

how big and heavy the monstrous beast must be.
Heracles followed its tracks, but old spoor crossed
with new and it was often difficult for the hero to decide which set he should follow. He walked for days,
climbing mountains, clambering down gorges, losing himself in forests, till in the end, walking round
a rock, he suddenly saw the lion before him. It was
huge beyond belief, with a great shaggy mane and
wild eyes which seemed to dart fire. Heracles crept
unseen behind a bush, unslung his bow and took
aim at the lion's forehead. The arrow hit the beast
between the eyes, but it merely shook its head and
scratched the place with its paw as if it had been bitten by an insect. Heracles shot a second arrow, twice
as hard, and hit the lion in the throat. But again, it
was as if the arrow had struck a stone; it rebounded
and the lion slouched off in a bored manner and
disappeared behind a rock. Heracles ran after it, but
when he reached the spot the lion was nowhere to
be seen. Heracles searched the area in bewilderment
till he spotted the entrance to a cave. From the paw-
marks at its mouth he realized this must be its lair.
Concealing himself behind a large boulder, he sat

down to wait, but night fell and the beast had still not reappeared. "He is sure to come out in the morning," the hero told himself, and when dawn rose he was waiting impatiently, poised to strike it down with his club. But the sun rose higher in the sky and the lion showed no sign of coming out of the cave. Then suddenly there came a terrible roar, louder than Zeus' thunderclaps, echoing and re-echoing among the mountains and the gorges. Heracles turned in its direction and finally made out the lion, a tiny dot on the mountain opposite.

"How did the lion leave its lair without my seeing it?" the hero wondered. "It may have been a dark night, but I would still have seen it, or heard it, at least. Perhaps I dropped off to sleep without knowing. Now I must wait here till the beast returns. If I go in search of it, the way is long and difficult, and it will be gone before I reach the spot."

Heracles kept watch for three days and three nights, but still the lion did not come back to its lair. The hero was losing hope, and had half made up his mind to go out searching among the hillsides and ravines once more, when he heard a noise behind him. Turning his head, he saw the lion coming out of its cave.

"There is something strange here," thought Heracles. "Here was I waiting for the beast to go back into its den, and now I see it coming out!" It was then he realized there must be a second entrance to the cave.

While the hero was coming to this conclusion the lion arched its back and, like a springy rod bent back and suddenly released, it sprang through the air and in a few great bounds had disappeared from sight.

Heracles had lost the lion again, but he was not dismayed. He went straight off in search of the second entrance to the cave, and when he found it he quickly blocked the hole with boulders so huge they were impossible to move. Having done this, he returned to the first entrance to await the beast once more.

Suddenly, as dusk was falling, a terrible roar was heard, followed by a second and a third. The roaring came from far away and showed that the lion had gone to the other mouth of the cave, found it blocked, and was now giving vent to its fury. When it finally reached the first entrance, night had fallen. Heracles realized it would not be wise to face the monster in the dark, so he let it enter its lair unchallenged and waited in hiding for dawn to break.

When the sun came up, he approached the entrance to see if it would be possible to fight the lion in its den. But the roof of the cave was too low for him to bring his club down on the beast with any force. Nevertheless, Heracles decided to make his way a little further in, hoping he might at least hear something. And he did – from far away came the faint sound of hideous roaring and confused grindings and thuds which showed that the lion was trying to unblock the other entrance. Hearing this, Heracles left the cave and ran round to its second mouth. A moment later, one of the huge boulders he had heaved there toppled from its place, but the hero was ready and waiting. Tossing a mass of dry branches into the opening he immediately set fire to them, and the wind was blowing in just the right direction for all the smoke to go billowing into the cave. Running straight back to the first entrance, Heracles hid behind a rock, confident that the beast would appear now. Sure enough, it was not long before the lion

came out. It was obviously in distress, and its eyes
were red and streaming from the smoke, but it was
still a formidable adversary. Peering suspiciously
around, it sensed the presence of foe. Opening its
mouth wide it let out a savage roar, displaying all
its fearsome teeth. Its tail lashed its body in fury
and its paw struck the earth with such force that the
ground trembled with the weight and strength of the
blow. But however frightening the monster might
have seemed, Heracles was not daunted. Lifting his

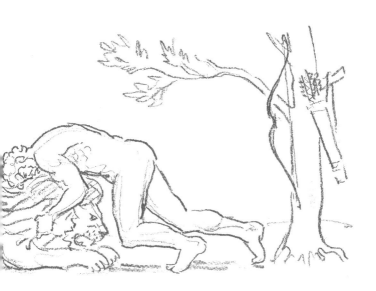

club high above his head, he suddenly stepped out
from behind the rock and, before the beast had time
to make the slightest move, he brought a shattering
blow straight down upon its skull. But not a bone
in the beast's head was broken, while the iron-hard
olive club was split from top to bottom, so mighty
were the two opposing forces it had come between!
Heracles had not struck in vain, however, for the
hitherto invincible lion of Nemea was now so dizzy
it could hardly stand on its feet. Tossing away his

club, the hero hurled himself on the beast's neck, holding its head in such a vicelike grip that it could neither bite nor tear him with its claws.

Now the Nemean lion's fate was sealed. It tried to shake Heracles off but to no avail. His great muscles squeezed the monster's neck in an ever tightening grip till finally it choked, and its black soul went to the dark depths of Hades.

Heracles rose to his feet bathed in sweat, exhausted but happy. He had killed the lion of Nemea; the first labour was accomplished. All that now remained was to take the body back to Mycenae and fling it in the courtyard of Eurystheus' palace. He tried to carry it on his shoulders but the burden was a heavy one and the road to Mycenae long and hard. Heracles had no alternative but to skin the beast and take the pelt to Eurystheus. Yet how could he strip the skin from the body when not even the keenest sword would pierce it? The answer came to him when he saw the lion's claws. Pulling one of them from its paw he skinned the lion with ease, threw its pelt over him like a robe and set off for Mycenae.

Meanwhile, further along the way, a man carrying

a load of wood was walking slowly, bent down by his burden and his sorrow. At the end of the path he was on there stood a little hut. On reaching it, he threw the wood to the ground and sighed deeply. It was Molorchus, and he had brought the wood because next morning he would have to make a funeral sacrifice for Heracles, who had not returned although a month had passed.

Night was falling, so Molorchus went into the hut and lit a fire, not so much to see by as to heat his soup. Just as he was taking the pot from the hearth, the doorway was darkened by the towering mass of a man wrapped in the skin of some wild beast. He looked so savage in his strange garb that Molorchus shook with fear, but the friendly tone in which he bade him a good evening soon calmed the poor man sufficiently to invite the stranger to sit down and share his dinner with him.

As soon as he was seated, the newcomer asked Molorchus:

"Have you heard the news? The Nemean lion is dead and gone. Now its soul is rotting in Hades and we can graze our flocks in peace once more."

But instead of looking pleased, Molorchus gave a deep sigh.

"Aren't you glad to hear the news?" the stranger asked in surprise.

"No, I'm not," came the answer. "I don't know whether what you say is true or not, but one thing I am sure of: Heracles is dead. That's why I've got that pile of wood outside – to light his funeral sacrifice in the morning."

"In the morning we shall sacrifice together to our guardian, Zeus. Bring a burning stick, my friend, and take a closer look at me."

At that moment it began to dawn on Molorchus who the stranger was. Snatching up a flaming branch from the fire, he let the light play on the other man's face. It was indeed Heracles who sat before him, and what is more, the hero was clad in the pelt of the Nemean lion. Speechless with joy, the poor man flung himself into his arms and kissed him, tears streaming down his cheeks. Then he took the whole bowl of soup and placed it before Heracles.

"I'm not hungry," Molorchus told him. "I've eaten already."

But Heracles was not deceived by this.

"Bring me another bowl, will you," he asked; and when the simplehearted fellow had brought one the hero poured out half the soup for him. Long after they had finished eating, a fire still lit the inside of the poor hut as Molorchus sat with bated breath listening to Heracles recount his incredible feat.

In the morning they both rose early and offered sacrifice together to almighty Zeus; then Heracles bid farewell to Molorchus and set off once again for Mycenae.

Covered from head to foot in the Nemean lion's skin, the hero made his appearance at the gates of the palace. When Eurystheus set eyes on him, his blood froze in his veins. His fear on first seeing Heracles was nothing compared to this. He fled panic-stricken to his room to escape from the sight of this "wild man", but there another horrid shock awaited him. For he had hardly managed to get his breath back when the door opened and two soldiers came in bearing the pelt of the Nemean lion, stretched out wide for Eurystheus to see.

"Heracles told us to give you this, great king,"

they announced. But before they could finish speaking, their brave king had fallen to the ground in a dead faint! When he came round, he was in such a lamentable state that he was only fit to be put to bed again. When he eventually fell asleep, Hera appeared to him in a second dream and told him what task he must set Alcmene's son to ensure that this time he did not return.

As soon as Eurystheus awoke, he called his herald Copreus and commanded him to go straight to Heracles with orders to kill the Lernaean Hydra.

And as Copreus was leaving, he shouted after him:

"While you're about it, take this damned lion skin and give it back to its accursed hunter!" And let that be the last I see of both of them, he told himself. He may have killed the lion of Nemea, but he'll never come back alive from the place I'm sending him now!

The second labour: The Lernaean Hydra

Now the Lernaean Hydra, as we said before, was the dead lion's sister. A venomous and ugly monster,

... "*Heracles told us to give you this, great king,*"
they announced ...

it lived in the Lernaean swamp spreading death and destruction throughout the region. No one had ever dared to hope that a man might one day be found to despatch it, for the beast had nine heads, and one of these was immortal. And even if the attempt were to be made, the monster had its lair in the depths of the swamp, where nobody could approach it. Besides, when it did come out it hid in the water and the reeds, from where it could fall upon its unsuspecting victim or on any would-be hero foolhardy enough to go in search of it.

Heracles decided to go to the Lernaean swamp in his chariot, taking his nephew Iolaus with him; for he was a bold young man and an able charioteer. As usual, the hero was armed with club, sword and bow, but this time he also wore the pelt of the Nemean lion.

"What a fool Eurystheus is," he told Iolaus. "He fears me and longs for my destruction, and yet he gives me back this lion skin which is not only proof against all weapons, but even against the Hydra's venomous teeth. And worse for him, now he's made a gift of it, he cannot ask it back."

When they got close to the swamp, Heracles climbed down from the chariot and told Iolaus to wait there with the horses.

"I am going to search for the Hydra," he added.

"Let me come, too," the young man eagerly offered.

"No, that cannot be," the hero replied. "I must go alone to kill it. Eurystheus has made this a condition. I know he is determined to send me to my death, but I must abide by the rules he has set."

Heracles began his search. It needed great care, for at any moment the monster might rise to the surface, and at every step he risked sinking into the inescapable clutches of the swamp.

Eventually he made out the monster's lair in the distance. It lay by a spring, in a completely inaccessible spot. However, something was stirring in the reeds, and Heracles was sure the monster was there. The problem was, how to lure it out of the place where it was lurking, and onto solid ground.

But no problem was insoluble for Heracles. He stood there pondering for a moment, then gathered some dry branches and lit a fire. Setting his arrow-

heads alight in its flames, he took up his bow and
fired them into the rushes around the monster's lair.
They immediately flared up, and the furious Hydra
came hissing out of its shelter; but wherever it went
the reeds around it were showered with Heracles'
burning arrows and burst straight into flame. Now
only one way was left for the Hydra, and there her
enemy stood firmly planted. The monster did not
hesitate; one bite, and he would topple lifeless to the
ground – for from her fangs there poured the most
deadly venom in the world.

Wild with rage and hissing horribly, the Hydra
sped through the water to the spot where Heracles
stood, scrambled up the bank and threw itself upon
him. But the hero was ready – and covered by the
lion's skin. Bringing down his keen sword, he began to lop the monster's heads off one by one. All
the while, the Hydra was biting furiously, though,
strangely enough, without result. Not only that, it
was breaking its teeth in the attempt. But then all
monsters are stupid, and so the Hydra could not
understand that it was not Heracles she was sinking
her teeth into, but the pelt of her dead brother from

*... one bite, and he would topple lifeless
to the ground ...*

Nemea.

Even so, things were not easy for the hero. To his
amazement, he saw that while he seemed to have
cut off most of the monster's heads, it now had
even more than before. And then he noticed that for
every head that fell, two more sprouted in its place,
opening wide their hideous mouths and threatening
with their teeth. Granted, they were no longer any
danger to him, for by now the Hydra had wearied
of breaking her teeth on the lion's pelt – but on the
other hand, the harder Heracles worked to cut off the
monster's heads, the faster they grew, getting him
nowhere. Worst of all the Hydra had succeeded in
winding its tail around the hero's leg and was trying
to bring him down. It would have been easier to
uproot an ancient oak tree than the son of Zeus, but
even so it made his task more difficult, and he realized that with his sword alone he would not be able
to defeat a monster such as this. While he was trying
to find a way around the problem, he felt a sharp nip
on his foot and looked down in alarm, not troubled
by the pain but by the thought of the Hydra's poison. When he saw what had bitten him, however, he

relaxed once more, for it was only a crab. This crab, a giant one, it is true, had been sent by Hera to help the Hydra when she saw that it could no longer bite, but Heracles pierced its shell with a single thrust of his sword, killing it instantly. Disappointed, Hera took the crab and placed it in the heavens. And that is how the constellation of Cancer is said to have been formed.

Now Hera, of course, had sent the crab to do harm to Heracles, but its nip actually worked to his advantage; for the clever hero realized that this gave him the right to seek aid in his turn. And so he called out to Iolaus, telling him to rekindle the fire and sear the bleeding stumps of the monster's necks with burning brands each time he cut off one of its heads.

The young man rushed to do as he was told and indeed it stopped new double heads from growing. One by one Heracles lopped them off until only the immortal head was left. Using all his awesome strength, the hero dealt it one final blow with his sword and the hideous thing fell heavily to the ground.

Helped by Iolaus, Heracles then dug a deep pit

and flung the head into it, still hissing viciously and baring its sharp-edged teeth. After that they filled the pit with stones and over it they rolled a huge boulder that no one would ever be able to move. For even though it had been severed from its body, the head was still highly dangerous.

And so the invincible monster was finally defeated. Heracles breathed a deep sigh of relief and satisfaction. From now on the people of all the surrounding region would be able to go about their daily work in safety.

Accomplishing this second labour again worked to Heracles' advantage. For tearing open the dead body of the Hydra, he dipped the heads of his arrows one by one into her venom. Whatever tasks Hera's favourite might set him in the future, he was now well armed to face them. Once more, the miserable Eurystheus had not only failed to do the hero harm, but had unwittingly done him a favour. For now Heracles possessed the deadliest weapons ever known to man: the arrows steeped in the Lernaean Hydra's poison.

Last of all, Heracles and Iolaus gathered up the monster's fallen heads from where they lay scattered on the ground, stuffed them into a sack and made for Mycenae. When they reached the palace, Eurystheus not only refused to look at them, but set up such a howling he could be heard throughout the city.

"He'd poison me, the villain! Tell him to take them away from here at once and bury them; yes, bury them miles away! I command it!"

Eventually he calmed down and his fear and anger left him – only to be replaced by a deep melancholy. For it was becoming clearer with each labour that Heracles was a hard man to put down – maybe impossibly hard.

The third labour: The Stymphalian birds

But yet – in the lake of Stymphalia there lived some hideous birds of prey which had laid waste the surrounding countryside. Their wings were of bronze, their beaks and claws of iron, and they were both immense and bloodthirsty. Neither man nor beast could approach the lake, for as soon as the birds saw either they would shower them with bronze feathers as heavy and sharp as arrows, then

dive on their wounded victims and devour them.
Such were the terrible Stymphalian birds, and,
guided once again by Hera, Eurystheus commanded
Heracles to destroy them.

The hero set off for the lake accompanied once
more by Iolaus. As before, he was protected by the
lion's pelt, while the young man carried a huge
shield. When they reached Stymphalia, everything
was silent. The birds were nowhere to be seen. But
on the ground there lay some large feathers, some
sunk deep into the earth.

Heracles picked one up, looked at it with interest,
weighed it in the palm of his hand and said:

"It's made of solid bronze. What an arrow!
Imagine what these can do when they fall like rain.
But don't worry; your shield is strong and all you
need is a little care. And I have the lion skin, so
nothing can harm me."

The trouble was, all the birds were roosting in their
nests and there was not one to be seen. Eventually,
two did appear. They launched a few bronze feathers at random, but had no time to perfect their aim.
Two of Heracles' arrows sent them tumbling from

the sky and they were swallowed by the waters of the lake.

But the problem was not to be solved by shooting down the odd bird or two as they appeared. The region had to be cleared of them forever, and report had it there were so many that they were beyond all count.

As Heracles stood there, beginning to realize just what a difficult task he was faced with, there came the sudden thud of something heavy hitting the ground beside him. A moment later it was followed by another.

"Rattles – two of them!" exclaimed a bewildered Iolaus. "They've just fallen from the sky!"

Heracles picked one up. It was made of bronze and was much like the wooden rattles villagers used to scare birds from the fields, only larger.

"Athena has sent us aid in a difficult hour!" cried Heracles. "These will get the birds up off their nests! Pick one up, Iolaus, and swing it round, like me!"

And the two of them began to whirl the rattles round in the air.

The noise they made was terrifying. The

Stymphalian birds, which were roosting in the nearby rocks, rose in alarm and circled, shrieking, in the air. In an instant the sky was filled with the vile creatures, and to the noise of the rattles was now added the clashing of their brazen wings and the harsh cries which issued from their throats. It was a chaos of hideous sounds.

"Enough with the rattles!" Heracles cried, and seized his bow.

Not one of the hero's arrows missed its mark. Many of them even brought down two birds at a time, for the venom of the Hydra in which their tips were dipped meant that the merest glancing scratch was enough to kill. Lifeless from the sky they tumbled, some to be swallowed by the green waters of the lake, some crashing into the reeds and others thudding onto the rocks below with a clash of brazen feathers.

Heracles wreaked havoc among the Stymphalian birds with his bow. They tried in vain to fell the two men with a shower of metal darts, but both Heracles and Iolaus were well protected from the bronze feathers which rained down on them. Soon

... Not one of the hero's arrows missed its mark ...

the whole area was littered with the corpses of the birds, and then the remainder, croaking with fear, took to their wings and were quickly lost over the horizon. The fearsome birds of prey had left lake Stymphalia for ever. Flying over land and sea, they finally reached a desert island in the Black Sea and never returned again. Lake Stymphalia was clean and safe once more, and with the departure of the flying monsters, smiles returned to the lips of the people who lived in the region.

But there was one set of lips to which this brought no smile at all. Eurystheus fell into a frenzy of rage when he learned that Heracles had come back alive. But Hera comforted him with these words: "Heracles has twelve labours to perform, and he has accomplished only three. You may be sure that in one of them he will meet his death. Command him now to bring you back alive the savage boar which runs wild on Mount Erymanthus. It is so fleet-footed that he will never be able to catch it."

Then Hera bent down and whispered in his ear the other dangers that Heracles would face before he found the boar. And Eurystheus rubbed his hands in glee.

The fourth labour: The Erymanthian boar

When Heracles received his new orders he was puzzled. Why should the mean-spirited Eurystheus send him to perform this task? True, the boar was a ferocious beast and whenever it came down from the mountain it wreaked havoc in the fields and garden-plots, rooting in the earth and ruining the farmers' patient labour. And if any body had the bad luck to catch it at its work, it would fall on them with its razor-like teeth and kill them in an instant.

However, Heracles knew how to protect himself. The only problem was how to catch the beast alive – but he would find a way.

Obviously Eurystheus had not commanded the hero to bring back the boar because he felt sorry for the inhabitants of the region. But if not, then why had he sent him?

Still turning this question over in his mind, Heracles set off for Erymanthus. A few days later he reached the foothills of the mountain. It was high noon, and he had stopped by a spring to drink some water and take a rest when he heard hoofbeats

approaching. He got up to look and saw a rider gal-
loping towards him. But when the "rider" drew near,
the hero's jaw dropped open in surprise. For this was
no man on a horse, but a centaur, half human and
half horse. And the name of this centaur was Pholus.

When he caught sight of Heracles, Pholus came
trotting up, gave the hero a friendly greeting and
asked him what he was doing in these wild parts.
Heracles told him who he was and why he had come
there, and the centaur was delighted at the acquaint-
ance, for he had heard of the hero's deeds.

"I would be honoured if you would come to our
cave," he said, "to share a bite of food with me and
rest your legs. Let's go now, before my brothers come.
I'd rather they didn't learn you'd passed this way, for
they're a rough lot, and have become the terror of
the region. Only Cheiron is calm and friendly – but
then, he's wiser than the gods themselves. Yet no one
listens to him, and even those who escape the boar
do not escape from us. It's a god-forsaken place, I
tell you, and nobody sets foot here if he can help it.
But anyway, come and eat something. I wish I could
ask you to stay longer, but I'm afraid of what might

happen with my brothers. If they're in the mood, they could kill you just for the fun of it."

When they reached the cave, Pholus proved a good host. He set Heracles down and served him tasty food. Only food, however, no wine.

Yet in the corner there was a great jar of wine, so why hadn't he been served any? Heracles put the first morsel in his mouth, then he could contain himself no longer.

"The food is delicious," the hero remarked, "but I'm afraid that without wine it just won't go down."

Pholus was ashamed by this and felt sorry that he hadn't given the hero anything to drink. Yet there was a reason.

"We centaurs," he said, "have the finest wine in the world. But we do not even offer it to the gods. In your case I will make an exception – though heaven help us if my brothers get wind of it."

And with these words he filled two goblets and gave one to Heracles. As the pair of them drank, the air was filled with the sweet and heady fragrance of the wine.

The smell was sweet, but its consequences were

bitter.

So strong were the fumes that they wafted out of the cave, where a little breeze, sent by Hera, carried it away and into the nostrils of the other centaurs.

"That's the smell of our wine!" cried the first.

"They're drinking our wine!" the second shouted.

"They're stealing it, you mean!" a third one cried. And with that they all set off for the cave at a gallop.

Pholus was the first to hear their hoofbeats, and he rushed out to look.

"We're lost!" he cried in terror. "They've got wind of us, and they're coming!"

When he heard this, Heracles ran out to join him.

As soon as the other centaurs saw a man outside their cave they flew into an even greater rage. Immediately they armed themselves with whatever lay at hand, some with huge boulders, and others with whole cypress trunks which they uprooted on the spot. Then they came charging down on the cave, and Heracles found himself in mortal danger.

One centaur alone, the wise Cheiron, tried to hold them back – but in vain. A moment later they began to hurl their great stones. Luckily, the distance was still too great, and they fell short of Heracles, who immediately drew his bow and began shooting with strength and accuracy. His arrows, dipped in the poison of the Lernaean Hydra, threw the centaurs into confusion. Every shot brought one of them down, as if he had been struck by a thunderbolt. Cheiron cried out to them to stop, but no one listened, and one after the other they fell lifeless to the ground. When the last few survivors saw the incredible outcome of the brief battle, they took to their heels and scattered in all directions. Eventually, some found refuge in Malea, while others, like the centaur Nessus, settled in the region of the river Evenus.

Though all the fierce centaurs were either slain or pursued from Mount Erymanthus, there was no joy in the battle for Heracles, but only great sorrow.

For one of the hero's arrows pierced a centaur's arm and flew on to strike wise old Cheiron in the foot. Now of all the centaurs, only Cheiron was immortal, but the Hydra's venom opened such a hideous wound that the pain was beyond endurance. Heracles himself ran to wash the wound, but he knew it could never be healed. Sure enough, Cheiron suf-

fered years of agony, till in the end he begged mighty
Zeus to let him die that he might escape from his
endless tortures. Zeus heard the centaur's plea, but
he did not let the god of death take him down into the
dark depths of Hades; instead, he took Cheiron up
into the heavens and placed him in that constellation
which has ever since been called The Centaur.

Yet old Cheiron was not to be the only friend that
Heracles mourned that day. Grieved at the loss of
his brothers, Pholus bent down, picked up an arrow
from the earth and asked the hero:

"How can such a tiny arrow bring death so
quickly?"

"Do not touch it!" Heracles cried out in alarm, so
loud that Pholus dropped the arrow with a jerk. In
falling, its pointed tip just grazed the centaur's leg.
But that was enough. Pholus sank to the ground,
dead – such was the power of the Lernaean Hydra's
poison.

Grief-stricken, Heracles buried his centaur friend,
then left that cursed spot and made his heavy-hearted
way up Erymanthus in search of the wild boar.

Now he realized why Eurystheus had sent him to

this place. He could not harm the hero physically, of course, but he had dealt a cruel blow to his heart. The death of Pholus and Cheiron's long-drawn agony would weigh heavily on Heracles' spirit for many years to come.

But sorrow or no sorrow, his mission was to hunt the boar and bear it back to Eurystheus.

After searching far and wide, Heracles eventually tracked the beast down. It was easy enough to kill, but his orders were to catch it alive, and here was where the problem lay.

The hero pursued the boar for days and nights on end, but it ran as fast as lightning, burrowed into thickets and wormed its way through clefts too narrow for Heracles to follow. Time and again he would lose the beast, wear himself out finding it and set off in pursuit once more – all to no avail. Yet somehow it had to be caught. Heracles at last sat down and thought. Strength and speed were not always the answer; sometimes cunning was needed, too, and in this quality the hero was not lacking.

"I must drive the boar to a spot where it cannot escape me," he decided.

Climbing a high rock, Heracles gazed all around him. Finally, his eyes were drawn to the snow-clad peaks of the mountain. "Yes, that's where I shall make him go," the hero said, and began to hunt the boar again, forcing the beast ever higher. Whenever it tried to veer off course, he would throw stones in its path, obliging it to go the way he wished. And so he drove the boar up among the peaks, finally forcing it into a hollow filled with snow. Buried in the fluffy, white mass, the animal's wiry little legs could no longer carry it forward. Its heavy body sank to the chest in the snow and there it foundered, unable to go on or retreat.

So, at last, Heracles caught the boar, tied its legs together, heaved it backwards across his shoulders so it could do no harm, and took it back to Mycenae.

With long, firm steps, Heracles strode past the startled guards at the palace gates and, quite by chance, ran right into Eurystheus. As soon as the latter set eyes on the hero with the wild boar on his shoulders he let out a piercing shriek and his legs turned to jelly beneath him. And then a scene unfolded which became a favourite theme of ancient

... the mighty king of Mycenae leapt into the air and straight into the open mouth of a great clay jar ...

Greek vase painters. In his terror, the mighty king of Mycenae leapt into the air and straight into the open mouth of a great clay jar. As if nothing unusual had happened, Heracles strolled over and bent down over its rim to let Eurystheus have a closer look – so close that the beast's snout with its needle-sharp teeth all but touched the craven braggart's face. Cold sweat poured from his limbs; he trembled like an autumn leaf and turned almost as yellow. Had Hades opened beneath his feet he would not have been so frightened.

The fifth labour: The Ceryneian hind

It took Eurystheus nine whole days to recover from the shock of seeing the wild boar, so for the first time, Heracles did not set out at once to accomplish his next labour, but rested for a while to regain his strength. And the truth is, he needed every moment of it. But on the tenth day, Copreus the herald summoned him with new orders from his master: to find the Ceryneian hind, sacred to Artemis, and bring the uncatchable beast back to Mycenae alive.

"Now this fellow shall see what it means to run and never stop," said Eurystheus to himself, delighted at the thought of Heracles running himself into the ground to no avail – for he was sure that this time he would succeed in humiliating the hero.

"And if he should catch it, so much the worse for him!" Eurystheus gloated. "For then he will have to face the goddess Artemis, who loves the hind and watches over her – Artemis the cruel, who knows no punishment but death."

It was indeed true that Artemis loved the hind above all other creatures. It had been a gift from Taygete, daughter of Atlas and mother of Lacedaemon, one of the first kings of Sparta.

The Ceryneian hind was the swiftest and most lovely creature in the world. She could run without ever tiring, for her hooves were made of bronze, while her head was adorned with splendid antlers of solid, gleaming gold.

For a whole year Heracles pursued her – over mountains, through gorges, across rivers, chasing after her down the sides of valleys and across broad plains. He crossed the isthmus of Corinth, panting after the hind to the peaks of Cithaeron, Parnassus and Oete, then hunted her down into Thessaly and on into Illyria. Sometimes he ran under a burning sun and sometimes in biting frost. At times he would bruise his feet on sharpedged stones, at others flounder through soft snow. The Ceryneian hind led him ever onwards, beyond the sources of the Istrus and up into the lands of the Hyperboreans; then back again to Greece and down into the Peloponnese, outrunning him over the Artemisian mountains and across the breadth of Arcady. The sacred animal showed no sign of tiring and Heracles followed doggedly behind, never losing sight, but never getting near enough to catch her.

Until they reached the river Ladon. Here, at last, the hind stopped in her wild flight and looked around her for a place to cross. And Heracles, seeing there was no other solution, bent his bow and took aim at her legs. His aim and timing showed all his skill in archery, for his arrow passed through all four legs at once, at the very moment they came together in a leap, passing between the tendons and the bones, and drawing not a drop of blood. The deer was not badly hurt, yet she could not move an inch when Heracles ran to catch her.

But before he could even get his arms around the hind, a woman's voice echoed through the deserted spot.

"How dare you!" it exclaimed.

And spinning round, Heracles saw Artemis, the great goddess of the woods, her bow aimed straight at him and uncontrollable rage written all over her face.

Now the hero knew that the hind had been a gift to Artemis. He also knew what a formidable goddess she was, and how unmercifully she punished all who did her the slightest harm. He remembered how harshly she had dealt with Actaeon for a completely unintended offence; how she had revenged herself on Niobe by killing all her children without pity and how she had even found a way of destroying the Aloades when those fearsome giants threatened to topple the gods from their thrones.

Heracles knew all these things; yet he was not afraid.

"How dare you!" exclaimed the goddess once

again. "How dare you wound my hind? A whole year you have been in pursuit, and I left you alone, for I knew you were not swift enough to bring her down with your bare hands. But chasing her was not enough – you had to wound her, too! Just who do you think you are? Zeus may be your father, and I your sister, but you are no god, and I shall not have pity on you. Explain this insult, and explain it

quickly – for my arrows never miss!"

"I am obeying the orders of Eurystheus, the fool-
ish little king of Mycenae. I shall lead this hind back
to his palace, show it to him, then set it free once
more. It was not I who decided to do this, but the
gods themselves. And as you see, I respect the gods
and carry out their wishes. Now, if you think I have
acted wrongly, kill me."

Artemis was startled by his reply. "If you think I have acted wrongly, kill me," Heracles had said. Yet he had obviously acted rightly. On the other hand, he had wounded her hind, and the goddess took this as a great insult. Two forces struggled within her: on one side was her Olympian pride, and on the other simple logic. For a while longer she stood thoughtful and undecided, but in the end she lowered her bow and said:

"Take the hind to Eurystheus, only be careful not to do her further harm. This is the first time a man has made me bend my will. You are to be congratulated, Heracles."

So Heracles took the hind and led it to Mycenae. For strength, speed and even cunning are not always enough to accomplish great deeds. Sometimes dignity of spirit is required as well – and that was a quality Alcmene's son had never lacked.

As for the mean-spirited Eurystheus, he foamed at the mouth with rage when he learned that this labour, too, had been carried out successfully.

"Yet there is a way to keep this Heracles from my palace gates," he thought, "and to humble and shame him utterly, as well. I'll set him to shovel dung for the rest of his days!" And immediately he called his steward:

"Copreus! Copreus! Send Heracles to clean the stables of Augeias!"

The sixth labour: The stables of Augeias

Now the stables of Augeias, king of Elis, were piled mountain – high with stinking dung which had never once been cleared away.

This king Augeias was the son of Helios, the sun god, and he possessed innumerable animals, both large and small. Among them were three hundred fine black bulls with white legs, a gift from Helios himself, another two hundred as red as the setting sun, and twelve more as white as swans. Outstanding among them all was a bull which shone so brilliantly it might itself have been the great god of the day.

Apart from his flocks and herds, Augeias also owned all the most fertile land – and strangely enough it was the very richness of the plain of Elis which had caused the problem the region was now facing. The fields were already so fertile they could take no manuring – and so the dung was never removed from the stable yards, where it piled up, year after year, until it stood in heaps so high no man could shift them. If all the people of Elis, down to the last woman and child had laboured in the stables night and day for years, they would still not have been able to clear the evil-smelling mass away. That is how much dung had gathered in the stables of Augeias, and there it lay, spreading pestilence across the whole region.

This mountain of manure had to be cleaned up somehow – and what is more Heracles was obliged to do it alone.

"Let him wallow in the muck his whole life through – and let him die in it," Eurystheus gloated. "And then we shall see who is worth more: a great king like me, or a lost hero subjected to my will."

As soon as Heracles reached Elis, he went to inspect the stables. When he saw the task which lay before him, the envy and resentment little Eurystheus harboured for him were made clear once again.

"But there must be an answer to the problem," he

told himself, and sat down to think of one.

After a while, the inklings of a plan began to form in his sharp mind, and he immediately jumped up and ran to the top of some rising land which over-looked the surrounding countryside. From there he could make out two rivers which wound across the plain to left and right like two huge, shining snakes, before losing themselves on the horizon. The stables lay between the Alpheius and the Peneius, the big-gest rivers of Elis and all the Peloponnese. Heracles took a long and careful look at them, then came down the hill again, smiling, and went in search of king Augeias.

"I am Heracles, son of Alcmene," he announced when he had found him, "and I have come to clean your stables."

"Got enough workers, have you?" the king asked ironically, "because I can't spare you any."

"I need no workers," Heracles replied. "I shall clean them out myself."

Augeias laughed. "And how many years do you think you're going to live? Thousands?"

"I shall clean your stables in a single day," replied

the hero in a confident voice.

"Now listen, Heracles, if you're going to talk with me, talk seriously!"

"But I am being serious – quite serious. Your stables shall be cleaned in a single day."

"If you do what you say, then you shall have a tenth of all my herds," was the king's reply; and calling his son Phyleus he told him to witness the agreement.

Then Phyleus demanded that Heracles swear on oath that the stables would be cleaned before nightfall, and although the hero had never sworn an oath before, he did so now.

"And you, too, father," Phyleus continued, "swear that if Heracles can do what he has promised, you will give him one tenth of your herds."

Augeias swore in his turn, and the next day, Heracles began work at dawn.

When the sun was high in the heavens, Augeias went to his stables to see how the work was proceeding. But there was no sign of Heracles and not the slightest indication that anything had been done.

"Why did I bother to come to this stinking place?"

he said with a shrug. "I knew his words were the words of a madman, yet I sat here and sealed a bargain with him – and with oaths and witnesses as well."

"Your majesty," a shepherd said, "I saw Heracles down at the Peneius."

"His work's here and he goes down to the river? What was he doing there, anyway?"

"Don't ask me!" the shepherd replied. "Crazy things. He's throwing earth and stones into the water – huge rocks, even. Incredible strength! He's got more muscles on him than a titan. But what's the use? Now if he stayed here for a few years, then perhaps he might be able to do something."

"I told myself he was crazy – and how right I was!" the king replied. "Now, let's get out of here before the stench knocks me down." And they all left hastily, with their hands over their noses.

The shepherd had been right. Heracles really was working down at the rivers. He was building two dams. By midday the work was finished and masses of water began to rise up behind them.

"Soon the water will have risen high enough to

overflow exactly at the spot I want," said Heracles; and he ran to the stables, where he made two large openings in the wall which surrounded them. As soon as this was done, he climbed to the higher ground nearby to wait and see what would happen.

He did not have to wait for long. "The waters of the Peneius are coming!" he cried in triumph. And a moment later, "and now they're coming from the Alpheius!" Indeed, before long, the waters of the two rivers came surging into the stables through the gaps in the walls and did their work so quickly and so well that Heracles was beside himself with joy. He had not only cleaned the Augeian stables but washed them out besides. A better job could never have been done.

Heracles then went down to the rivers again, demolished the two dams, came back up to the stables and repaired the breaches in the walls. His task was completed. As the sun sank behind the western hills, the hero returned to Augeias.

Now the king had already learned what had happened, but instead of being pleased he was furious, for he had no wish to hand over the beasts he had

... A better job could never have been done ...

promised to Heracles.

"It wasn't you who cleaned the stables!" he shouted. "It was the rivers!"

"Just what do you mean by that?" asked the hero in surprise.

"I mean that the work was done by the river gods, Alpheius and Peneius. They're the ones I owe my thanks to!"

"And you owe nothing to me? What about our agreement?"

"We made no agreement!" the king retorted.

"Then what about your oath?"

"I gave no oath at all!" Augeias shouted, beside himself with rage. "Now get out of here, you cattle robber!"

Heracles could not believe his ears. The man's insolence knew no bounds. It wasn't the loss of the promised animals which troubled him, but Augeias' double-crossing was more than he could bear. The hero decided not to let the matter drop, but brought him to court.

The judges called Phyleus as a witness and the young man bravely told them the whole truth about what had passed between Heracles and his father. Heracles won his case, but Augeias sprang up in a fury and not only refused to accept the judges' verdict but exiled both them and his son – forbidding Heracles ever again to set foot in Elis.

"I shall return," retorted the hero, "and you will pay dearly for your dirty tricks. I would make you pay on the spot, but this is not the time. The gods have pressing work for me to do, but I shall not forget, be sure of that!"

And nor did he. When the twelve labours had all been accomplished, Heracles returned to Elis with an army. He fought and killed Augeias and in his place made Phyleus king. Heracles did not wish to take the cattle he was owed, so Phyleus offered him a stretch of land by the river Peneius in their stead. There, Heracles built a temple to Olympian Zeus and a great stadium, which people say he measured out by the length of his own stride. He named the spot Olympia and in it he organized the first Olympic Games.

When Heracles returned to Mycenae, Eurystheus was taken completely by surprise, for he had never expected to see the hero again. Trembling with fear, he called Copreus and ordered him to find out how Heracles had come back when he had sent him off on a task that should have taken a thousand years and more to complete.

"I have already learned, great king," was Copreus' reply. "He cleaned the stables of Augeias in a single day!" And then he went on to explain just how Heracles had performed that seemingly impossible labour.

The steward's words threw Eurystheus into still greater panic, for now it was clear to him that Heracles was not only strong and brave, but exceedingly clever as well. The mean and slow-witted king of Mycenae felt that he was a mere nothing in comparison, and this made him feel an even deeper longing for the hero's downfall. But this was easier said than done: Heracles always managed to emerge victorious. He had throttled the Nemean lion, slain the Lernaean Hydra and cleared Lake Stymphalia of its birds of prey. He had brought the Erymanthian boar back to Mycenae, captured the Ceryneian hind, and now he had cleaned the stables of Augeias. Half the labours were accomplished, and each had seemed a task beyond human achievement. What was to prevent him from carrying out the rest? Eurystheus was tortured by this thought, till Hera came to his aid once more and advised him that the remaining labours could be made even more formidable if Heracles were sent off to distant regions to face new challenges. The first six tasks had all been in the Peloponnese; the next six would require long and often dangerous journeys.

The seventh labour: The Cretan bull

Indeed, the seventh labour was doubly perilous. Eurystheus ordered Heracles to catch the fearsome bull which was ravaging the fields of Crete – and not only to catch it, but to bring it back alive across the sea to Mycenae.

But first of all, what kind of creature was this Cretan bull?

King Minos of Crete had once promised the god Poseidon that he would sacrifice to him whatever beast was cast up living on his shores. And so in due course Poseidon caused a splendid bull to be washed ashore in Crete, a bull with golden horns and hooves of bronze.

But when the great king saw the superb creature, he broke his promise to the sea god and kept it in his stables. And in place of Poseidon's bull, he sacrificed an ordinary one.

Poseidon was mortally offended.

"Does Minos hold the gods so cheap?" he cried out in his rage. "Does he hope to profit by keeping the bull against my will? Well, he will soon see what he gains from it – nothing but misfortune and grief!"

And suddenly the splendid bull, till now as placid as a lamb, was turned into a raging monster. Possessed by a wild urge to destroy, it attacked man and beast alike, leaving a trail of carnage in its path. All who tried to tame the creature or destroy it were killed in the unequal struggle; for the bull's mad rampage was an expression of the sea god's wrath.

Now there fell to Heracles the task not only of catching the beast but bringing it back alive to Mycenae across the broad Aegean.

The hero sailed to Crete and sought king Minos' leave to carry out the task.

"I'm quite willing," replied the king, "but I doubt if the bull is! And you say you want to take it back across the sea? You must be out of your mind! Well, I hope you succeed, but even if you don't, I won't shed any tears over you. One hero the less is no great loss to the world."

"How they all hate me, these kings," said Heracles to himself. "Eurystheus, Augeias, and now Minos. Well, so be it. My job is to catch the bull and take it back to Mycenae."

It did not take long to find the creature, and the fight began at once. For as soon as the bull caught sight of the hero, it charged with lowered horns. The thunder of its approaching hooves was enough to arouse terror in any man, but Heracles stood firm, darting aside only at the very last moment, as the bull made its final lunge. Instead of the expected target, its horns met empty air, and, as its knees buckled, were driven headlong into the ground by the sheer force of its charge. In a flash, however, the bull was on its feet once more, and, with a hideous bellow, launched a second attack upon the hero. But for all its efforts, the maddened beast had spent its forces in

that first lunge, and this time Heracles stood firm as
it threw itself upon him. Just as the bull's head was
about to strike home, Heracles seized its horns in a
grip of steel and stopped it in its tracks. A shudder
ran through the animal's mighty frame, as if it had
collided with a wall of rock.

With all his awesome strength, Heracles forced
the bull's head downwards till its nostrils scraped
the ground. The beast struggled wildly, but in vain:

try as it might, it could not lift its head again. Its rear hooves scrabbled desperately in the earth to gain some purchase, but nothing could dislodge the son of Zeus or make him lose his balance. Foam bubbled from the bull's mouth in its impotent rage, but there was nothing it could do. Soon, the last of its strength was spent and it gave itself up to its opponent without further resistance.

Then Heracles tied a rope around the bull's horns.

When the beast regained its forces, it made no attempt to free itself or set upon the hero. The fearsome bull of Crete had been tamed at last.

And so Heracles led the bull down to the sea. Now, the task which had once seemed impossible had suddenly become more than easy. Instead of swimming to the Peloponnese with a maddened beast upon his back, Heracles did just the opposite: he let himself be carried there, sitting comfortably upon the beast's broad shoulders.

When they reached its shores, Heracles led the bull to Mycenae and haltered it in Eurystheus' stable. But when the king learned that the terror of all Crete was tied up in his farmyard, he cried out in dismay and ordered his men to drive it up into the mountains, as far away from Mycenae and his palace as they could. While Heracles had overcome the bull and brought it back safely tied, Eurystheus set it free again out of sheer cowardice. Little he cared what revenge the enraged beast might wreak on his people!

Once more at liberty, the bull became the terror of the Peloponnese. Eventually it crossed the isthmus of Corinth and made its way to Marathon, where it ravaged the countryside around. Now known as the bull of Marathon, it was later destined to be killed by Theseus, the great hero of Athens.

The eighth labour: The horses of Diomedes

After the journey to Crete, and again following Hera's advice, Eurystheus next sent Heracles to Thrace, to bring back the horses of king Diomedes.

These dangerous beasts the king kept locked up in his stables, bound with heavy chains. Their jaws were said to be of bronze, and their sole diet human flesh.

But still more to be feared than his horses was Diomedes himself, who ruled the savage Bistones. A son of Ares, god of war, the love of battle was in his blood. Whenever he led his warlike tribe into combat, it meant ruin and destruction for his unfortunate neighbours.

Even greater than his lust for destruction was his pride in his man-eating horses. Whatever prisoners fell into his hands were fed to them alive. It was not only his captives in war who met this dreadful fate, but every unsuspecting stranger who passed through Thrace, believing that here, too, the rules of hospitality laid down by Zeus himself held good. Of all the strangers who fell into the hands of Diomedes, not a single one escaped; his man-eating stallions devoured them all.

When Heracles set out for the land of the ferocious Bistones and their bloodthirsty king, he took with him a number of friends who were ready to fight at his side if the need arose. Among them was Abderus, a daring youth from Locris.

The hero and his companions reached Thrace by sea. Heracles soon learned where the horses were stabled, and while his comrades fell upon the guards and bound them, he quickly unchained the beasts from their stalls and holding them by their bridles, he led them down to the ship.

"Stay here while I get the horses on board, and give me a shout if you see Diomedes coming!" Heracles told the others. But despite his orders, Abderus ran after the hero, in case he needed help. Before they had even reached the ship, they heard shouts.

... holding them by their bridles,
  he led them down to the ship ...

"Diomedes! Diomedes is coming with the Bistones!"

Heracles hesitated for a moment, and Abderus knew why.

"Don't worry," he said, "you can leave the horses with me."

Heracles was none too happy at the thought, but he had no other choice. Leaving the animals with Abderus, he ran back to face the danger. Still distant, but approaching fast, he saw a countless horde of Bistones, led by Diomedes on a black charger. As they came on, they shouted fiercely and brandished their long spears.

Heracles and his comrades were in deadly peril. How could so few of them hope to withstand so many? But the hero found an answer.

He noticed that the plain on which they stood lay below the level of the sea, which was held back by a wall of sand-dunes thrown up by the waves.

"Come on! Help me open a channel so we can flood the plain!" he shouted to his companions; and before the words were out of his mouth he was digging furiously.

Soon they had made a breach in the dunes – narrow at first but quickly widened by the inrushing sea. Before long, a broad mass of waters was rushing over the plain to form a great lake. The lake is still there today, and its name is Bistonis. Many of the attacking Bistones were carried away by the foaming flood; the remainder took to their heels. Diomedes and his retinue, who were out in front, escaped the rushing waters but their retreat was blocked and they now had Heracles and his comrades to face.

Caught like beasts in a trap, they turned at bay to meet the heroes' attack but were soon cut down. Diomedes himself was knocked from his horse by a blow from Heracles' club. He was not killed, but instantly held and bound – and for a good reason: the cruel king deserved to be paid back in his own coin, and so he was fed alive to his own horses.

The enemy were defeated, but Heracles and his friends had suffered a sad loss. The savage horses had torn Abderus to pieces, and there are no words to describe their grief at the death of the brave young man.

Heracles was inconsolable.

"It was my fault for leaving him alone," he kept saying. Yet everybody knew the hero had had no choice.

Heracles asked his comrades to give Abderus a splendid burial. And so they sacrificed the finest animals that could be found, then honoured their dead companion with athletic contests. In order that his name should never be forgotten, they built a city in that place and called it Abdera.

When the heroes had at last fulfilled their debt of honour to the young man's memory, they boarded their ship and set sail for Mycenae with the horses.

When they reached the port of Argos, however, Eurystheus forbade Heracles to bring the animals down to Mycenae. Instead, he was to set them free again.

"Let him take them anywhere he likes!" cried Eurystheus, in a voice tremulous with fear, "but keep them away from me and my palace!"

To prevent the horses from doing any further harm to men, Heracles took them far away to a remote slope of Mount Olympus, where they were eventually devoured by wild beasts.

The ninth labour: Hippolyta's belt

When the hero returned to Mycenae a new command awaited him. He was to bring back the belt of Hippolyta, queen of the Amazons. Once again, the idea was Hera's.

The goddess was even more vexed than Eurystheus to see that Heracles had achieved success in every labour set him. Something still more difficult must be found – that is why she thought of the Amazons, and Hippolyta's belt came into her mind. Then she recalled that Admete, the king's daughter, was a priestess in her own temple. She could easily fill the girl's head with a longing to possess the Amazon queen's belt for herself. So, when the princess next went to worship in Hera's temple at Argos, the goddess appeared before her and said, "Admete, daughter of Eurystheus: there is a magic belt worn by Hippolyta, the renowned queen of the Amazons. It was given her by Ares, god of war, and is a symbol of authority and power. You could wear this belt yourself, if you were to ask your father to command Heracles to go and bring it."

Admete was delighted with the idea of acquiring such a belt; and Eurystheus was more delighted still when his daughter asked the favour of him. Without losing a moment, he called for Copreus and said:

"Tell Heracles to bring back Hippolyta's belt!" But to himself he said something quite different: "I hope the fellow never returns and my daughter never gets the belt!"

When Heracles received the order to carry out this task, he immediately realized how difficult it would be. Once more, he decided to make the journey by sea, with a group of brave companions. Yet again, the most famous heroes in Greece showed their willingness to risk their lives at Heracles' side. Among them were Theseus, the great hero of Athens, Iolaus, who was Heracles' nephew, the bold young Telamon from Salamis and Peleus, who later became the father of Achilles.

Their ship set sail with a fair wind and made its first landfall on the island of Paros – where they also encountered their first danger.

Now the king of this island, which lies in the Cyclades, was a certain Alcaeus and on the day when Heracles' ship sailed in, he happened to have three sons of king Minos with him as his guests. They were proud, hard and inhospitable men, though they themselves were guests in a foreign land. As there was no water left on board, Heracles sent two of his comrades on shore to fill the jars. And there, in spite of the sacred laws which protected strangers in need of food or water, they were set upon in stealth by the sons of Minos and killed.

Heracles witnessed the scene from the deck, and bursting with rage and indignation he jumped ashore, followed by his companions. The sons of Minos paid for their crime with their lives, but the fighting soon swelled into a battle with the inhabitants of the island. Heracles and his comrades beat back the islanders, however, and forced them to take refuge within their city walls.

When the Parians realized they had started a war against the mighty Heracles, they soon admitted their mistake. Two heralds mounted the ramparts and blew their trumpets as a signal that they wished to speak. Then one of them shouted out, "Heracles, son of Amphitryon, our king Alcaeus had no wish for this war. He was deeply grieved when he learned that fighting had broken out between us, and that the sons of Minos had murdered your two men. He now proposes that you choose two Parians, the bravest you can find, and take them with you on your expedition."

Heracles' reply surprised them all.

"Give me king Alcaeus and his brother Sthenelus. These two are your bravest men, I think."

A deadly hush fell at his words. Nobody knew what would happen next. But soon the great gate of the castle opened, and Alcaeus and Sthenelus came out with firm and steady step and stood at attention before Heracles.

"At your orders!" they cried together.

Instead of issuing commands, Heracles folded the two men in his arms and kissed them. Two young and valiant companions had taken the place of those that had been lost, and soon the ship set sail for the land of the Amazons.

Travelling northwards, Heracles and his comrades made passage through the Hellespont and the Bosporus and came out into the Black Sea.

Following the coast of Asia Minor, they landed in Mysia, where king Lycus gave them a hearty welcome. A sumptuous feast was laid out in the great hall of the palace. On one side sat king Lycus with all the lords of Mysia, and on the other Heracles with his band of heroes. But while they were eating and drinking and proposing toasts to one another, a soldier came running into the hall. He seemed to have travelled a long way, for he was bathed in sweat and coated with dust from head to foot.

"Your majesty!" he cried out to king Lycus. "The Bebrycans have invaded! They have smashed our resistance and are headed for the capital, killing, burning and looting everything in their path."

The whole company rose to their feet. Lycus looked in consternation at his nobles, who had turned a sickly pale.

"If we are to die, then let us die fighting!" he cried.

"Alas! We are lost!" was all the nobles could reply. "What will become of our wives and children?"

Heracles cut short their despairing cries.

"Courage!" he shouted in a ringing voice. "You are not alone. Forward, comrades! Into battle!"

And with these words, Heracles and his companions charged out of the palace and went forth to meet the foe. Soon they were in the thick of battle. With their appearance, events took a sudden turn. The vigour of the heroes' attack spread panic and confusion among the Bebrycans and lent new courage to Lycus' men. The enemy were defeated, their monarch killed and a large part of their country ceded to Mysia. In his gratitude, Lycus named the region Heracleia. When the time came for their quest to be renewed, Lycus gave the bold adventurers as many provisions as their ship would hold, while a vast crowd came down to the harbour to bid them a farewell fit for gods.

Heracles' ship sailed onwards, and after a long voyage it reached the mouth of the river Thermodon. It entered the river, and the heroes soon caught sight of Themiscyra, capital of the Amazons.

Heracles leaned on the tiller and studied the city as the ship slowly drew closer.

He had heard a great deal about the Amazons.

It was said that the first of them had been the children of the war god Ares. They learned the arts of war from their father, and in turn taught them to their children – or rather to their daughters. For they kept their menfolk solely for household tasks while they spent their time learning to fight with sword, lance and bow, mounted on swift-footed horses. They became famous for their valour all over the world. No army on earth could withstand the renowned Amazons. They mounted expeditions all over Asia Minor and into the Caucasus. They ventured south as far as Syria and westwards to Thrace and the islands of the Aegean sea. They are even said to have reached as far as Libya. The inhabitants of many cities, among them Ephesus, Smyrna, Cyrene, Myrina and Sinope, claimed with pride that their towns had been founded by the Amazons.

Now these warlike women lived in the region surrounding the river Thermodon. They were divided into three tribes and had three cities, with Themiscyra as their capital, ruled over by queen Hippolyta. The other two cities were governed by Melanippe and Antiope.

Heracles' ship had now come close to the shore, where a crowd of Amazons had gathered, many of them on horseback. Perhaps it was mere curiosity that had drawn them there – or perhaps it was foreboding.

This expedition had not appealed to Heracles from the start. He had no wish to make war on the Amazons to take from them something which was rightfully theirs – or rather their queen's.

"I must persuade Hippolyta to give me the belt of her own accord," he told himself, "just as I persuaded Artemis to let me carry off her hind to Eurystheus."

A few moments later their ship cast anchor. Heracles went ashore first. Hippolyta was among the crowd, and the hero distinguished her immediately. She too knew who the rugged stranger was who had leapt down from the ship so boldly, for Heracles' exploits had made his name renowned throughout the world. To show her high regard for him, Hippolyta got down from her horse to greet the hero.

When Heracles saw the queen close up he was astonished. For Hippolyta was burnt a deep brown by the sun, and her arms and legs rippled with muscles. Even men as strongly built as this were hard to find.

And all the other Amazons were the same. Heracles' companions stared in wonder.

At a loss for words, the hero raised his hand in greeting.

Hippolyta did likewise, adding, "Heracles, son of Alcmene, tell us whether you come in peace or for war. If in peace, we welcome you; if for war, we are ready to oppose you."

"I came here with no thought of war in mind," the hero replied. "I did not even come here of my own accord. It is the will of the gods that I perform twelve labours – and not those of my own choosing, but those commanded by Eurystheus, king of Mycenae, a cowardly and mean-spirited man who hates me like the plague. He sent me here – to take the belt you wear."

Hippolyta was startled when she heard the purpose of Heracles' voyage. A troubled murmur ran through the ranks of the Amazons. Then a deathly silence fell. They were all waiting to see what answer Hippolyta would give.

But instead of giving an answer, the queen asked a question.

"And Eurystheus sent you here to take my belt because he believed you would never get back alive. Is that not so?"

"They are your words, not mine," Heracles replied, "but you have guessed correctly. Yes, it is so."

"Then Heracles, I give you my belt, so that you may take it back to Eurystheus," said the queen, and put down her hands to release it from her waist.

But at that moment the goddess Hera stopped Hippolyta from giving away her belt. She transformed herself into an Amazon, and just as the

queen was holding it out to Heracles she cried:

"No! We must not give up the belt. This fellow came to carry off our queen, and he must die!"

Hippolyta drew her hand back as angry war-cries broke out among the Amazons. Bows were drawn. An arrow whined through the air. The dauntless Aella had aimed straight at Heracles. Once again the Nemean lion's pelt saved the hero. The arrow struck the impenetrable hide and rebounded harmlessly. But now it was war! With a look terrible to behold, the son of Zeus bore down on the over-bold

Amazon; and when Aella saw the fierce lust of battle
in his eyes, she fled before her foe for the first time
in her life. Fleet-footed though she was, Heracles'
arrow laid her dead in the dust. In the meantime,
however, the bloodthirsty Prothoe had thrown herself on three of Heracles' companions and killed
them in an instant. She had no time to savour her
triumph, though, for the son of Zeus cut her down
at once. Then seven more Amazons charged on the
hero with their lances poised, determined to pierce
him through and through. Wielding great blows with
his club to left and right, Heracles killed them to
the last one. Nearby, Theseus, Telamon, Alcaeus
and Sthenelus were wreaking havoc among the
Amazons. Faced by the united heroes, these warlike creatures finally tasted defeat and fled. But not
before Heracles had made Melanippe his prisoner,
and Antiope been captured by Theseus. Beaten at
last, the Amazons begged for peace.

Hippolyta came forward to speak with Heracles,
but she was so overwhelmed that she could not utter
a word.

Heracles laid down his terms.

"You shall give me your belt, and Melanippe will be given back her freedom. This I grant because she is my own prisoner. As for Antiope, Theseus captured her, and I do not have the right to order her release. He will take her with him to Athens."

Hippolyta accepted. Heracles took the belt, Melanippe regained her freedom, and Antiope was carried off by the Athenian hero.

Theseus wondered why Heracles had not kept Melanippe, for she was as lovely as a goddess. He was on the point of asking, but the hero knew what was in his mind and forestalled the question.

"No, Theseus. I have the blood of a horrible crime to wash from my hands. It is not enough to perform the labours the gods have commanded me. I must not forget for a moment why it is I do them. Only thus will my unjustly slaughtered children ever be able to forgive me."

Then the heroes all boarded their ship and began the long voyage back.

On their way they had to put in at Troy, which was then ruled over by king Laomedon. As they rounded the harbour mouth, they beheld an incredible sight – a beautiful maiden tied to a rock, with the waves breaking at her feet. They soon learned the reason why.

It seems that some time before, Zeus had commanded Apollo and Poseidon to build the walls of Troy, as a token of his high regard for Laomedon – a regard which was, alas, misplaced.

The two gods undertook the task with heavy hearts, for they had heard that Laomedon was a hard and ungrateful man. To put their suspicion to the test, they appeared before him not as gods, but as ordinary mortals, saying that in exchange for a hundred oxen they would build a city wall that no army could ever breach.

Laomedon accepted their offer, but when the wall had been built and the gods demanded their payment he refused them, and in the vilest fashion.

"Remove yourselves from my presence this instant," he cried, "before I bind you hand and foot and sell you into slavery!"

"So this is Laomedon!" the two gods told each other. "Just as we thought!" And they decided to punish him harshly.

... As they rounded the harbour mouth,
they beheld an incredible sight ...

Apollo brought a plague upon the city, while Poseidon brought a sea monster to its coasts which devoured all who approached the shore.

Seeing there was no end to their troubles, the despairing Trojans consulted the oracle to learn how they could be saved from the disasters which had fallen on them.

The answer they received was this: their sufferings would only be ended if Laomedon's daughter, the lovely Hesione, was given to the sea monster to devour.

Now Hesione was the only creature in the world whom Laomedon loved, and he refused to give her up. In her place, he ordered that three girls should be chosen from the common people and eaten by the monster, so the curse would be lifted from the city.

Not one of the citizens would accept this unjust ruling, and they all hid their daughters from the king.

All Laomedon could find was the three girls of a poor man named Phoenodamas, and these he attempted to take by force.

But Phoenodamas defended his daughters with courage. The king could not wrest them from him unaided, nor could he find anyone to help him.

In the end, it was decided to cast lots among all the maidens of Troy. But here again, fate chose Laomedon, for the lot fell upon Hesione. There was nothing more the king could do. He gave up his daughter and she was tied to a rock to be torn to pieces by the frightful monster. This was the sight that met the heroes' eyes as they entered the harbour of Troy.

When Heracles heard the story, he offered to kill the monster himself but on one condition, for he wished to see if this time Laomedon would be as good as his word.

"If I succeed," he told the king, "you must give me the two horses which are harnessed to your chariot."

Now the horses which Heracles demanded were splendid, snow-white steeds, a gift to Laomedon from Zeus himself.

The king of Troy agreed, although he shook his head in despair. Nobody believed that a man could be found to kill a monster such as this. For all that, Heracles slew the hideous creature and the hero Telamon ran to untie the lovely Hesione and carried her tenderly to the shore.

However, so dishonest and ungrateful was Laomedon that this time, too, he refused to give what he had promised.

Heracles was filled with bitter rage, but he held himself in check.

"You will pay dearly for this," he warned the king. "Now I have other duties to fulfil, but I shall not forget you. I shall be back, with an army, and woe betide you then!" With these words he took his comrades with him and went aboard their ship.

Everyone was angry at what had happened – except for Telamon. The young man had fallen in love with Hesione. As they left, he turned and gazed into her eyes. And when Heracles made his grim promise to return, Telamon's heart was filled with joy. He would be among the first.

The companions' next port of call was Thasos. There they found that a savage tribe from Thrace had overrun the island and was terrorizing the inhabitants. Heracles made war upon these tribesmen and drove them out. Then he left the island in the hands of Alcaeus and Sthenelus, the two brothers he had brought with him from Paros. It was a fitting reward, for they had fought bravely at his side.

Heracles and his remaining comrades then set sail for Mycenae. When they reached the harbour the other heroes bid farewell and set off for their homelands while Heracles, belt in hand, made his way to the palace of Eurystheus.

Although the cowardly little braggart had forbidden Heracles to appear in his presence, this time the hero entered without asking anybody's leave. Nobody dared put out a hand to stop him. He made straight for the great hall, flung wide the double doors and marched in carrying Hippolyta's belt. The first person to set eyes on him was Admete, and when she saw what lay in the hero's hands she let out a cry of delighted surprise. When king Eurystheus turned to see the reason for his daughter's joy, he nearly dropped dead on the spot. A long, long time had passed since Heracles departed on his quest, so long that Eurystheus had come to believe that he had finally seen the last of him. Trembling with rage and fear, he began to shriek, "Out! Out!"

But it was Eurystheus who left first, by a little side

door which led down to the palace cellars. And there, when the worst of his fear had left him, the king began to ponder which mission to send Heracles on next.

With Hera's help, he found the answer.

The tenth labour: Geryon's cattle

He would despatch him to the furthest limits of the world, beyond the Great Ocean, to the island of Erytheia. There the cattle of the giant Geryon grazed, and Heracles would have to bring them back to Mycenae.

No other labour had yet placed the hero in such difficulties or danger. Eurystheus knew what fearful obstacles would have to be overcome and he was confident that this time he had seen the last of Heracles.

Geryon, son of Chrysaor, was a monstrous creature with three bodies joined together at the waist. He had three heads and six arms. He was as heavily armed as three warriors, wore three helmets, and protected his bodies with three shields so strong that not even the keenest lance could pierce them.

Now this Geryon had some cattle, the like of

which had never been seen on earth. They were a deep russet shade, with noble heads, broad fore-heads and slim, graceful legs.

Their herdsman was the giant Eurytion, and they were guarded by a savage watchdog named Orthrus, a brother of the dreaded Cerberus, who kept the gates of Hades. Orthrus had two heads whose jaws bristled with pointed fangs and a tail which ended in a dragon's head.

Geryon also had a voice of unbelievable power. It was said to have all the strength of the cry Ares once let out when he was wounded in the Trojan war – a howl as deafening as ten thousand warriors yelling together.

Whenever there was a violent thunderstorm, Geryon loved to shout with all his might, proud that his voice could drown the very thunderclaps of Zeus.

And at other times, when the air was calm, he would climb up on a rock above the sea and bellow with all his strength:

"Whoever wants the finest cattle in the world, let him come and wrestle me – and if he wins, they shall be his!"

The voice of the fearsome giant would ring out over the ocean to the distant shores. And if ever some brave warrior had hopes of beating Geryon and acquiring his marvellous cattle, he would go to try his strength against the giant – only to give Geryon the pleasure of killing him with ease.

Such was the formidable adversary whom Heracles would have to pit himself against this time; and there would be others, too, as we shall see.

The hero set out alone on this long and dangerous journey. After crossing Italy, he made his way along the southern shores of France then walked right across Spain, finally reaching the spot where Gibraltar stands today. Danger had faced him at almost every step in the form of robbers, monsters and wild beasts, all of whom he had fought and killed. It had been a hard journey, but a satisfying one; for now the regions he had passed through would be safe for travellers.

In those days, there was no sea passage at Gibraltar to the Great Ocean in the west. Heracles decided to open a wide channel for ships, and he laboured hard at this task. Whoever passes through the straits today will see two huge rocks, one on either side; they are said to be formed from the stones which Heracles piled up on the facing coasts to set as a landmark for sailors. These great boulders are called the Pillars of Heracles.

By the time he had finished the task, the hero was streaming with sweat, for the sun had been intolerably hot all day. So angry was he with the sun-god Helios that he drew his bow to frighten him, just as the god of day was finishing his journey across the skies and climbing into his golden boat.

"Lower your bow, Heracles," said Helios – not angrily, but admiring the hero for his courage. And in a kind voice he went on, "tell me where you are headed for – and if you wish my help, you shall have it."

"I am bound for the island of Erytheia," the hero replied, "to carry off Geryon's cattle and bring them back to Eurystheus, as the gods have commanded me."

"And how will you cross the Great Ocean?" Helios enquired.

"Give me your boat, and that question will soon

be answered," was the hero's reply.

Helios laughed at Heracles' ready retort, and he willingly gave him his boat.

"But do not take too long," he called, "for I must make my night passage and be in the east at the appointed time."

"I will return with all speed possible," said Heracles, jumping into the boat.

Helios' golden vessel bore him swiftly to Erytheia. Heracles tied it to a rock and stepped ashore. But he had not taken two steps when he was startled by a savage barking.

It was Orthrus, the monstrous two-headed dog which guarded Geryon's cattle. Baring its horrible fangs it bounded towards the hero, intent on tearing him apart. Heracles swung round, but he hardly had time to see what was happening before Orthrus was upon him. Had it not been for the lion's skin, those terrible teeth would have sunk deep into his flesh. But Heracles did not lose his nerve. He raised his club, and as the hideous beast leapt again he brought it down with such force that no second blow was needed.

The first threat had been dealt with, but now Eurytion came running to the scene. This herdsman of Geryon's was a giant twice the size of Heracles and with strength to match. The moment he saw Orthrus lying killed, he snatched up a huge rock to fling at Heracles. A single instant's hesitation and it would have been the hero's end. But a swift and well-aimed arrow struck Eurytion full in the chest, and the rock he had been poised to throw slipped from his grasp and crushed him.

Heracles hastily rounded up the cattle and drove them down to the boat. Since Geryon had not appeared, the hero did not intend to go in search of him. However, one of Pluto's herdsmen saw what was happening and went to warn the giant, who came running down to the shore to get back his cattle and punish the man who had dared to take them without wrestling with him first.

When Heracles set eyes on Geryon he stood rooted to the spot. Here was a sight to make the bravest quail. In one hand the giant grasped a sword, and in the second and third a lance. On his other arms his three great shields were slung. As he ran, his

weapons clashed together with such a din you might
have thought a whole army was advancing into battle. As he drew closer, he began to bellow war-cries
of such power that the heavens seemed likely to split
asunder. Anyone but Heracles would have fled at the
mere sight, let alone the earth-shattering noise.

Even the hero's courage wavered at that moment;
but he drew his bow resolutely, took careful aim and
fired. That shot was the beginning of the end for the
fearsome giant. One of his heads, and the great chest
that supported it, sank lifeless to one side. Two arms
sagged limply downwards while a lance and one of
the shields clattered to the ground. Now Geryon tried
to fling his second lance at Heracles, but his dead
arms got in the way, and his feeble throw fell short.
The hero's chance had come. Raising his club, he
dealt the giant a crushing blow on one head, quickly
followed by another on the second – and that was
the end. Geryon toppled dead upon the ground with
a mighty din of falling armour and weapons.

It was a victory greater than Heracles dared hope
for. Giving thanks to the goddess Athena who had
stood steadfast at his side, the hero drove the cattle

... Raising his club, he dealt the giant
a crushing blow ...

of Geryon aboard the golden boat and sailed back eastwards across the Great Ocean. When he reached the further shore, he returned the boat to Helios with his thanks and set out on the long and difficult journey back to Mycenae.

He passed through Spain again and entered southern France, where two bandits made off with his cattle. Heracles hunted them down, killed them both and took the animals back. But a little further on the road a third brother, Ligys, king of Liguria, set upon him with a whole army. He wanted both the cattle and revenge for his brothers' death. This was the most unequal struggle the hero had ever faced. He was fighting alone, his stock of arrows was soon exhausted, and worst of all the ground around was all soft earth, without a single stone to throw at his enemies. Heracles had never been in a more desperate position. He was wounded in several places, and was close to death. Now there was only one hope.

"Father Zeus!" the hero cried, "I have never asked your aid till now, but at this moment I need it as never before. Help me to defeat my enemies!"

And then almighty Zeus, in his great love for his

son, sent down from the sky a shower of stones, which Heracles picked up and hurled at his foes, saving both himself and the cattle. And indeed, between Marseilles and the mouths of the river Rhône there is a stretch of land called 'the Stony Plain' which seems to be the place referred to in the myth.

Leaving France and Spain behind him, Heracles drove the cattle eastwards into Italy. As he was passing through the region where Rome was later to be built, a giant named Cacus stole eight of the finest bulls and heifers, and, to prevent the hero following their hoofprints, dragged them away by their tails and hid them in a cave.

Before long, one of the cattle lowed and Heracles found their hiding-place. But Cacus had blocked the mouth of the cave with huge rocks which seemed impossible to move. Heracles managed to dislodge a boulder which formed the roof of the cave and thus uncovered it, but as he did so, Cacus reared out of the darkness, a hideously misshapen giant with hot flames belching from his mouth. For all his horror, Heracles attacked at once, while Cacus tried to burn him with his tongues of fire. But a swift and deadly sword-thrust to the giant's throat put out the flames in an instant and Cacus drowned in his own blood. Heracles drove the stolen cattle back to the herd and continued on his way – but his troubles were not over, for further on the way one of the animals broke loose from the rest, jumped into the sea and swam across to Sicily.

It would have been impossible for Heracles to search for the stray had not Hephaestus appeared before him at that moment and offered to guard the herd till his return.

So Heracles crossed over to Sicily where he found the missing animal in the herd of king Eryx. But when he asked for it, the king told him he would only give it back if the hero could beat him in a wrestling match. As no one had ever yet succeeded in defeating him, Eryx felt sure that he would keep the beast.

Heracles wrestled with the king and pinned him down. But Eryx refused to admit that he had been beaten, and would not hand the animal over. Then Heracles fought and beat him once again, yet still the king would not accept his defeat. Not till Eryx was killed in a third bout did Heracles get all his herd once more.

After many more hardships and dangers, the hero brought them back to Greece at last. It was no longer very far to Mycenae. But just when all Heracles' troubles seemed to be at an end, Hera set a gadfly on the herd. Its poisonous sting sent the animals stampeding wildly in all directions. The tireless hero chased after them – over the mountains of Thrace and to the Hellespont beyond. The pursuit was long and immensely arduous but finally Heracles succeeded in rounding up the herd once more and set off back again for Mycenae. When he reached the river Strymon, however, he found himself faced by yet another difficulty. The river was so deep and wide the animals could not get across. In his fury, Heracles flung so many boulders in its waters that the Strymon is no longer a navigable river.

The Strymon was the final obstacle in the hero's path; yet even when he had brought the cattle safely over he was still a long way from Mycenae. But distance was nothing compared with the dangers and the difficulties he had suffered up to now. So he set out on the last great homeward stretch, and finally reached the end of this terrible journey.

Eurystheus was now the owner of the most wonderful herd of splendid cattle, but they gave him no pleasure at all. Indeed, the sight of the beasts made him so miserable he sacrificed them all to the goddess Hera. To have sent Heracles to the very ends of the earth, through the worst of dangers and pitted against the most fearsome monsters, and then have him come back victorious – it did not bear thinking about. Where could he send him now? Could there be a task still harder?

The eleventh labour: The apples of the Hesperides

"Yes!" came Hera's reply. "We shall send him to bring three golden apples which he must pick from the tree the goddess Earth gave me as a wedding present. He can search as much as he likes, but he will never find that tree. He will wander all over the world like a hunted man, encountering such foes that he will never escape their clutches. And even should he learn of the place where I have hidden the apple tree, it is so safely guarded he will only lose his life in the attempt. For I have set the dragon Ladon to watch over it – the only monster in the world that can never be beaten, for it is immortal. Set off then, Heracles! Here is a labour crowned with glory – but a crown which you shall never wear, for the labour is impossible!"

"Yes, off you go, Heracles!" echoed Eurystheus. "Now we shall see which of us is the better man!" His voice had a confident and commanding ring. This was easy to explain: Heracles was not there to hear it!

The hero had to depart on this next labour without the least idea where he was going. No matter whom he asked, he could not gain a single piece of useful information. His aimless wanderings brought him into Thessaly where he came face to face with Cycnus, the bloodthirsty son of Ares and after with the god of war himself. He defeated them both in combat, killing Cycnus and wounding Ares, who took to his heels howling with pain.

After this Heracles continued on his way, crossing

Illyria and northern Italy until he reached the river Po. There on the river bank he found a group of nymphs and, as so many times before, he asked if they knew the whereabouts of Hera's apple tree. As he had expected, they could not tell him where to find this tree, which the goddess had hidden away from the eyes of gods and men. But they were able to tell him something else:

"The only one who knows where the tree you seek is to be found is the great seer, the old sea god Nereus."

"But will he tell me where it lies?" the hero asked the river nymphs.

"That he will never tell you," was their reply.

"How can that help me, then?"

"What can we say? We have told you all we know."

Now Heracles' problem was how to worm Nereus' secret from him.

"Can you tell me where I might find Nereus, at least?" he asked the nymphs.

"Certainly. Go down the river until it reaches the sea, and there you will find a cave. That is where the great seer lives. But what do you hope to achieve?"

"I shall wrestle with Nereus," said the hero, "and force him to tell me what I want to learn."

"Wrestle with him all you will," the river nymphs laughed, "but you will never defeat him."

"I have fought and vanquished the most fearsome monsters in the world," Heracles retorted. "You think I can't beat old Nereus?"

"If it were so easy to wrest the secret from him, Hera would never have entrusted it to Nereus alone. As soon as you lay hands upon him, he will turn into a snake and slither from your grasp. If you catch the snake, it will become a bird and flutter from your hands. And should you ever snare the bird, it will dissolve into water and be swallowed by the thirsty earth, or change into mere air and disappear. Don't waste your time wrestling with Nereus, for you will achieve nothing. Face the truth, Heracles – you will never find out where the tree with the golden apples is hidden."

The downcast hero bid farewell to the river nymphs and set out in search of Nereus – not that he hoped to gain anything, but there seemed nothing else to do. He found the sea-god in his cave, asleep.

"Just what I wanted," Heracles whispered, and picking up a rope which lay there, he bound the old seer, at first lightly, so as not to awake him, then more firmly, and finally so tightly that he roused him from his slumbers.

Nereus tried to get up, but he couldn't move an inch. Looking down at his body, he saw that he was tightly trussed with coils of rope from head to toe.

"What is happening?" he cried. "Who are you?"

"My name is Heracles, and I want you to tell me where the tree is with the golden apples, the gift which Mother Earth made to the goddess Hera when she married mighty Zeus."

"That I shall never tell you!"

"Then I shall never loose your bonds!"

And indeed, Nereus was so tightly bound he could not move so much as his little finger, let alone find the strength to transform himself into another shape. He tried, but it was impossible, and to untie the ropes himself was equally out of the question. For a while he was speechless with fury; then he began to consider his predicament.

"What did you say you wanted?" he asked the

... *"Just what I wanted," Heracles whispered, and picking up a rope which lay there, he bound the old seer ...*

hero finally.

"Tell me where I can find the tree with the golden apples," Heracles replied.

"Ask me whatever else you like, and I shall tell you," promised old Nereus, "but do not ask me that again!"

"Then stay here trussed up in these ropes!" the hero retorted. "I shall block the entrance to your cave with rocks and shut you up inside!" And with these words he began to roll a huge boulder across the mouth of the cave.

What else could Nereus do? He had no choice but to speak.

"You will find the apple tree you seek," he told Heracles, "in the Garden of the Hesperides. This garden lies on the very edge of the world, where Atlas, brother of Prometheus, supports the celestial globe upon his shoulders."

"At last!" Heracles cried. "I have learnt where I must go."

"Go to do what?" Nereus asked him.

"To pick three golden apples, as the gods have commanded me."

"But that is impossible."

"Impossible?"

"Yes, impossible," Nereus informed the hero. "For the apple tree is guarded by Ladon, a hideous dragon with a hundred heads. And you will not be able to catch it in its sleep as you did me, for I warn you that it never droops its hundred heads together, but only half of them at once. So it always has fifty heads bolt upright with their eyes wide open, flickering watchfully around lest any stranger set foot in the garden of the Hesperides. You cannot creep up unobserved, and if you did you would not get off with your life, for Ladon is unbelievably strong and quite invincible. And even if the gods were to lend you twice your present strength it would be of no avail, for Ladon is immortal, too."

That was all Nereus had to say. Heracles untied him and left feeling very depressed. He had learned where the tree was, but he did not know how he could take the apples when they were guarded by such a terrible monster. He did not know what to do. For the first time, he had no desire to go where duty led. In a mood of black despair he let his footsteps guide him where they would, and eventually found himself in the wild and rocky Caucasus.

As Heracles was wandering in the mountains he heard terrible groans coming from afar. He stopped and listened carefully. It was clear that someone was suffering the most painful torture and was in need of help. Then, stranger still, the hero heard women's voices calling out his name!

Heracles ran in the direction of the voices and climbed up on a rock to get a better view. From his vantage point he saw a company of women with their arms stretched out towards him, begging for his help. Now Heracles recognized them: they were the Oceanides, the daughters of silver-haired Oceanus. He ran towards them, but before he had gone more than a few steps he beheld the most dreadful sight. The titan Prometheus, mankind's most faithful friend, was hanging in chains, nailed to a rock and undergoing the most hideous and end-less tortures that god or man had ever known. And as the hero gazed upon the scene in horror, a huge eagle swooped down from the sky onto the hanging figure, its cruel beak wide open.

How Heracles killed the eagle and loosed the patient titan from his bonds is a tale we have told in another volume. It was the finest and most noble action of the hero's life.

But something else happened which we did not need to mention then, and it concerns our present story.

When Heracles had set Prometheus free, and was bidding him farewell, the titan asked the hero where he had been bound for.

"What can I say?" came the gloomy reply. "My whole life has been one long chain of great labours and great suffering. Not once did I lose hope – but now my spirit fails me." Then he sat down and told the titan all his troubles, adding, with a hopeless shrug, "after all, I suppose I must go and wrestle Ladon, whatever comes of it."

"Listen to me carefully, Heracles," Prometheus replied. "I am a seer and I know. As Nereus told you, the dragon which guards the apples in the Garden of the Hesperides cannot be defeated, for it is truly immortal. Do not try, for if you do you will forfeit your life. But tell me this: do you think you can bear the heavens upon your shoulders? I know it is a mighty feat I ask of you; till now, none but Atlas could support the burden."

"If need be, I can do it!" replied the hero decisively.

"Then hold the globe for Atlas and let him bring you the apples. He is no stranger to the dragon and will not be harmed. But be wary! Atlas is a cunning fellow – and I should know, for he's my brother. Make sure he does not leave you there to support the heavens forever!"

Prometheus' advice gave Heracles the answer he'd been looking for, and his mood brightened at once. There was a long journey to be made, right across the world from east to west, but the hero set off immediately, sure now not only of his destination but of what to do when he arrived.

As usual, dangers lay in wait for him upon the way.

Somewhere in Egypt, when he had sunk exhausted under a tree to sleep, he was surprised by soldiers, who tied him up and took him to Busiris their king.

After he had inspected the hero from head to toe, Busiris ordered that he be bound more tightly still;

and when this had been done, he said:

"Tomorrow we shall sacrifice you on the altar of Zeus Ammon."

"Why?" asked Heracles, amazed.

"Take him away!" was the king of Egypt's only reply.

The hero learned the reason that night, from his guards.

Nine years before, a great misfortune had struck Egypt. The earth would not bear crops, and gnawing hunger threatened to wipe out the people. And then, from Cyprus, there came a seer named Phrasius. Busiris summoned him and asked whether he knew how the curse could be lifted from the land.

"Each year you must sacrifice a foreigner to Zeus Ammon," was Phrasius' reply.

As soon as Busiris heard the Cypriot's words he grasped the opportunity and shouted to his soldiers:

"Seize this seer here! He shall be the first foreigner we sacrifice to Zeus Ammon!"

Poor Phrasius! He had no problem foretelling others' futures, but when it came to himself, a little common sense would have done him far more good than all his magic arts. They failed him completely, and that was the end of him. Now every year they sacrificed a foreigner – and this time it happened to be Heracles.

Next day, still tightly bound, the hero was carried off to the altar of Zeus, where a splendid ceremony was being held. There were crowds of people, soldiers, priests, princes and princesses and, on a high throne, Busiris himself. Cymbals clashed, hymns were sung and musical instruments played. It was a brilliant and impressive gathering.

But the celebrations came to a sudden and ugly end. At the very moment in the ceremony when the high priest was raising his knife to plunge it into Heracles, the hero flexed his mighty limbs and snapped his bonds like threads. Clenching his terrible fist in fury, he struck first the priest, then Busiris and last of all his son. All three fell dead upon the ground. The soldiers and the people were terrified. At the sight of the stranger's awesome strength, they all took to their heels. Not one of them dared face him. The sacred precinct emptied as if by magic and Heracles found himself alone. Free once more, he quietly resumed his journey to the Garden of the Hesperides.

As the hero travelled westwards through Libya, to the regions where the sun sets every night in splendour, he encountered a formidable giant named Antaeus. This creature was a son of Mother Earth, who, loving all her children equally, adored him, evil though he was. Antaeus was unbelievably strong, and he forced all strangers to wrestle with him to the death. In this he was aided by his mother, who, fearing lest her son come to harm, helped him as he fought in a way that did not show. The more Antaeus' body touched the earth, the more she renewed his powers; so her son never grew tired, however long he wrestled. The result was that he never lost a fight.

As soon as the giant set eyes on Heracles, he challenged the hero to fight him to the death. Not knowing that Antaeus drew his strength from Mother Earth, Heracles fought long and hard against him, but in vain. Time and again he sent him sprawling backwards in the dust, and each time it was worse, for the giant would leap up with suddenly renewed vigour and send the hero flying. Heracles was puzzled. Where did the giant find these instant bursts of power when a moment earlier he had been close to defeat and grovelling in the dust? Then the hero remembered that his opponent was a son of Mother Earth, and the longer he lay upon her breast, the more life he would draw from her. So, gathering the giant in his arms, Heracles lifted him high into the air and would not let him touch the earth at all. In his desperate struggle to break free, all Antaeus' strength seeped out of him. And the fearsome giant met his fate.

Thousands of years have rolled by since then, but mankind still recounts the myth of Antaeus. For he is a timely reminder that all who have their two feet planted firmly in the earth, all who build upon the truth and draw strength from the love of their fellow men are invincible; while those who do not have these sure foundations are doomed to defeat and extinction.

After his victory over Antaeus, Heracles pressed on westwards till he reached the furthest limits of the world. There, for countless ages, the titan

... So, gathering the giant in his arms,
Heracles lifted him high into the air
and would not let him touch the earth at all ...

Atlas had borne the crushing burden of the heavens upon his shoulders. His only companions were the Hesperides, daughters of Hesperus and Night. Nearby, in their garden, stood Hera's tree with its golden apples.

Atlas was puzzled, seeing Heracles in these distant parts, for no one ever ventured this far. He welcomed the hero and asked why he had made the long journey.

"I have come to pick three golden apples from the Garden of the Hesperides," was the reply. "For I must take them to Eurystheus."

"And how will you get them?" Atlas asked. "Do you know what guards the tree with the golden apples?"

"I know – and that is why I have come to you."

"And what can I do?" Atlas shrugged. "True, I would love to go and bring them to you. Even a moment's rest would bring me great relief. But there is neither god nor man can bear the crushing weight I carry on my shoulders."

"I can."

"If you could, I should be grateful to you forever.

But it cannot be – for if the heavens were to fall, the world would come to an end."

"I tell you, I can."

"You sound so sure, I am beginning to believe you. Very well, then, let us give it a try!"

A second later, Heracles was stooping at the titan's side, his arms and shoulders pressing up against the heavens. Atlas lowered his shoulders a little. Heracles flexed his body, arms and legs with all the strength he had. His awesome muscles rippled and stood out as hard as stones. His legs swayed for a moment, then found their balance. Atlas felt the weight leaving him and, bending a little lower, he was freed. To his amazement, Heracles was holding up the heavens in a firm and steady grip!

For the first time in countless ages, Atlas could breathe without restraint. Feeling lighter than a bird he ran off to the Garden of the Hesperides, treading on air. Soon he was back with the three golden apples, which shone in the sun. But he was in no hurry to take the heavens back on his shoulders. He had another plan in mind.

"Listen, Heracles," he said. "Why don't I take the

apples to Eurystheus? It will not take long, and as soon as I am back I will relieve you of your burden." And without waiting for an answer, he turned to leave.

Heracles immediately remembered Prometheus' warning. He realized that if he could not find a way to give the task to Atlas once again and take the apples back, he would be left there forever, holding up the heavens. Cunning can only be fought with double cunning, and so he said to Atlas:

"Take them, by all means. I like holding this weight – only I don't want to hurt my shoulder, so would you mind carrying the heavens for a moment while I put a cushion there?"

The unsuspecting Atlas put the apples down and took the globe up on his shoulders once again. This was what Heracles had been waiting for. He picked up the apples and went on his way leaving Atlas to bear his dreadful burden for all eternity.

Glad to have the golden fruit of the Hesperides safely in his hands at last, the hero set off back to Greece. Immensely long though the return journey was, it seemed to pass by in a flash. Mountains and

...."Listen, Heracles," he said. "Why don't I take
the apples to Eurystheus?"...

plains, deserts and forests, rivers and seas succeeded one another until at last Heracles found himself in sight of Mycenae. Even he could hardly believe that he had accomplished such a feat.

"I must deliver the apples to Eurystheus myself," the hero decided, "however loud he screams." And he entered the palace without waiting to be asked. Carrying the golden fruit of the Hesperides, he presented himself before the king.

Eurystheus' jaw fell open when he saw him.

"I don't want them! I don't want them!" he shrieked. "Take your apples and get out of here at once!"

"I know you do not want them," was Heracles' reply. "You hoped for something else, like every other time. I only want to know what task you'll find to send me on next."

Eurystheus turned as pale as a dish-rag and tried to speak – but he was so afraid that he couldn't utter a word. Only when the hero had left and the servants closed the door behind him did the king regain his voice. Running to bar the door more safely, he shouted, "I'll send you to the underworld, where no one ever comes back from. That's where you'll go!"

Eurystheus had spoken the first threat that came into his mind, but as soon as the words were out of his mouth, his eyes began to glitter with evil hatred.

"Yes, that's it!" he chuckled, "I will send him to the other world! I shall order him to bring back Cerberus, the fearsome dog that guards the gates of Hades."

That was the only labour that Eurystheus thought up by himself; and it was the most satanic. Heracles had performed so many other incredible tasks, and still escaped the kingdom of the shadows. Now he would be ordered there direct. "And go he shall, whether he wants to or not," said Eurystheus to himself, rubbing his hands in glee.

While the king was laying his plans, Heracles went and gave the apples to Athena, who took them back again to the Garden of the Hesperides. For that was where they belonged, and it was not thought good for them to be elsewhere.

The twelfth labour: Cerberus

On his return from Athena, the hero was summoned by Copreus who delivered his master's orders for the next, and final, labour: he was to descend into Hades and bring Cerberus back from there.

Heracles was not at all surprised when he heard where the cowardly little king was sending him now, for Eurystheus could not have found a surer way of despatching the hero to his doom.

Cerberus was yet another son of Typhoon and Echidna, which made him brother of the Nemean lion, the Lernaean Hydra, Orthrus, Ladon and many other hideous monsters. He was a dog with three heads, all surrounded by a mass of hissing snakes, while his tail was tipped with a dragon's head. Cerberus was immortal, and guarded the gates of Hades with ceaseless vigilance lest any of the dead escape and make their way to earth again. If any of them even approached the gates, Cerberus would tear them to pieces and gulp them down in an instant.

Heracles set off on this formidable labour wrapped in his lion skin and armed with bow and club.

To go down into Hades alive was incredible enough, but to return from there with Cerberus as a prisoner was beyond the bounds of the most fevered imagination. When Zeus learned of this last task set to his son he was deeply troubled, but there was nothing he could do save order Hermes and Athena to guide him on his way.

Entering by a cave on the slopes of Mount Taygetus, the three plunged deep into the earth, and after hours of walking untrodden subterranean paths they reached the banks of the sacred river Styx.

There they found Charon, who ferried the souls of the dead across its waters in his boat. Although he did not want to take the living Heracles aboard, when Hermes and Athena commanded it, he had no choice but to obey.

When they reached the other side, Cerberus immediately smelled live human flesh and came running to the gate. As a rule, he did not care at all who entered, but when he saw Heracles, tall as a giant and armed as well, he began to growl and bare his teeth. Yet he did not try to hurt the hero, and neither did Heracles make any move against Cerberus.

Athena had advised him to first seek the consent of
Pluto, king of Hades; if he failed to do so, he would
encounter insuperable obstacles.

The three of them went through the gates of Hades.

Athena and Hermes were immortals. They knew
the kingdom of Pluto well and were not moved by
what they saw. But Heracles, who was not a god,
could not remain unmoved. Courageous though he
was, he felt fear clutching at his heart. The kingdom
of Hades stretched before him, boundless and dark.
Instead of sky above, it was roofed by tall stone
arches and sombre vaults of rock. Sobs and groans
could be heard on all sides, echoing and re-echoing
till all the broad expanse was filled with sounds of
misery.

Heracles had only taken a few steps more when
the souls of the dead caught sight of him and fled.
All save the fearsome Medusa, the winged gorgon
whose hair was a writhing mass of snakes. Not only
did she stand her ground, but beat her wings in men-
ace, while the snakes in her hair gnashed their teeth
as she fixed her hideous eyes upon him. Heracles
knew that if their eyes met for a single moment it

would be enough to turn him into stone, and lifting his club he prepared to strike her down.

"Drop your club, Heracles," Hermes told him. "Medusa is dead now and a pale shadow of her former self. She can do you no harm."

Another of the dead who did not flee was the hero Meleager. He was dressed in shining armour, and as soon as he spotted Heracles he ran towards him, sword in hand.

Seeing him thus armed, the hero thought he had been sent to kill him by Hera and drew his bow in readiness.

When he saw this gesture, Meleager realized what was wrong and put his sword away, for harming Heracles was the last thought in his head.

"It would not even cross my mind to hurt you," he told the hero. "The dead cannot harm a living soul. And nor can you do any injury to me, for nobody dies twice. But there are other evils just as great, Heracles, and I have suffered the greatest misfortune that could ever befall a man."

And with these words he sat down and told his tragic story: how his mother, who had loved him as mother never loved a child before, had in the end sought to destroy him; and how this had led to battle with Apollo himself, the immortal archer whose arrows never miss their mark. Only such an encounter could have brought him down to Hades, for in all the ranks of friends and foes alike, there had never been a warrior such as Meleager.

Heracles had never heard a sadder tale, and it moved him so much that tears welled in his eyes.

But Meleager had not finished yet.

"There is one thing which still troubles me: I left my sister Deianeira in my father's house, unmarried and with no one to protect her. She is lovely as a goddess, but I fear she may fall into evil hands. Become her guardian, Heracles – or better still, take her as your wife."

"Set your mind at rest, Meleager," the hero reassured him. "I shall do whatever is best for your sister. Do not trouble yourself on that account."

Finally, after other unexpected encounters, Heracles presented himself before Pluto, king of Hades.

Pluto was astonished to see him and sternly asked

just what he meant by appearing alive and armed before him. But his wife, Persephone, who stood there at his side, looked on the hero with a more sympathetic eye, for she, too, had been fathered by Zeus, and this made Heracles her brother.

"Mighty ruler of the underworld," the hero explained. "I did not come here of my own accord. I was sent here by Eurystheus, to whom the great gods gave the right to command me as he pleases and exact my blind obedience. I have subjected myself to that cowardly ruler's will to wash off the stain of a terrible crime; and he has sent me to perform the most impossible tasks with one sole aim in mind: to bring about my downfall – for the very fact of my existence fills his heart with fear. But so far, all his efforts have failed, and that is why he has sent me to your dark kingdom, because, he says, he wishes to see Cerberus; though if he set eyes on that creature he would be so frightened that he'd not know where to hide. Be that as it may. For me there is no choice – I must take Cerberus to Mycenae."

Pluto looked very doubtful. How could he let the guardian of Hades go up into the world above? It was unheard of. But Persephone looked at her husband so pleadingly that after much thought Pluto finally said:

"Very well, you may take the beast – but only if you can tame him without using your weapons."

Tame Cerberus bare-handed! If Heracles risked that, he might find himself in the dark kingdom of the shades for ever. But at least permission had been given, however harsh the terms, and the hero accepted the offer with relief. "I can do it," he said in a determined voice and turned to go.

Pluto, however, shook his head as if in pity, while two tears stole down the cheeks of Persephone – tears which she hid, for it was not fitting for the queen of Hades to weep.

Heracles made straight for the gates. When he saw Cerberus, he laid down his club and bow but wrapped the protective lion's skin more tightly round his body. Once again, the pelt of the Nemean lion would save the hero, and once again Hera would have reason to regret she had sent him on that first labour.

As soon as Cerberus spotted Heracles approaching

... Heracles then tied a strong chain round his neck ...

the gates of Hades he leapt to the attack. He had let the hero in, but that did not mean he would let him out again. Yet even Cerberus' sharp fangs were unable to pierce the lion's tough hide and Heracles managed to seize him by the throat, just at the point where his three heads sprouted. He squeezed with all his might and all Cerberus' efforts to break free were in vain. He bit the hero's leg with the dragon's teeth at the tip of his tail, but in spite of the pain, Heracles did not loosen his hold. In the end, Cerberus could not resist the choking pressure and he gave up the fight, thus signalling to his opponent that he admitted defeat.

Heracles then tied a strong chain round his neck while Cerberus, now thoroughly subdued, let out beseeching howls and lowered all three heads.

For the return journey, Heracles took a different route, which led through the Elysian Fields, a very different place from the dark halls of Hades, and the home of all the dead who by their noble deeds have won the favour of the gods. Then, following the course of the river Acheron along an endless winding cave, he came out to the upper earth by Troezen.

But as soon as they emerged, Cerberus turned savage once again. The snakes around his neck hissed wickedly, his mouths filled up with poisonous foam which dripped upon the ground, and his eyes flashed blinding sparks like those thrown from the wheel when knives are sharpened. He tugged against the chain with all his force, and barking frenziedly tried to escape back to the dark depths of the cave and out of the intolerable light of day.

But Heracles was on him in a flash, his hands outstretched to seize his throat once more, and Cerberus knew there was nothing he could do to save himself. Bowing his heads once more he followed the hero meekly.

Mycenae was no longer very far and Heracles swallowed up the miles with great strides. The final labour was drawing to its close. And now he was in the palace yard! When the guards saw what a monster was following at his heels they stepped back in alarm and kept at a safe distance. Nobody dared oppose his entrance. "He shall see Cerberus whether he wants to or not," said the hero to himself, and entering the great courtyard he came face to face with Eurystheus.

A wail of terror was all the welcome the little
king could give to the great hero when he returned
from the last and most formidable of his labours. So
great was his fear that he leapt into the air and dived
into a great clay jar – the same one he had hidden in
when he saw the Erymanthian boar. But this time he
pulled the lid down over his head as well and stayed
shut up inside for three whole days, too frightened
even to open the cover and see what was going on
outside.

Heracles gave a scornful laugh when he saw
Eurystheus jump into the pitcher like a startled hare,
a laugh so loud that it carried far beyond the palace
walls. Then he took Cerberus back to the cave where
he had brought him out into the daylight and loosed
the chain from around his neck. Swift as a flash the
hideous dog was lost to sight in the subterranean
darkness.

Carefree at last, Heracles took to the road once
more, not heading for Mycenae this time, but for
Tiryns. Ten years had rolled by since he entered the
service of Eurystheus. Ten terrible years of hardship,

but filled with glorious achievements, too.

Now his bondage to Eurystheus was ended. He had fulfilled the wishes of the gods and won the forgiveness he deserved, staunchly enduring the worst to wash away the fearful crime he had committed when he slaughtered his own children in the grip of madness.

A HERO FOR ALL TIMES

Heracles defeats Charon

The twelve labours had been accomplished, but Heracles' great feats were not destined to end here. Indeed, it was not long before he was again required to prove his strength and valour by placing his life in danger. And this happened when he had gone to seek a little rest and relaxation!

When Heracles had set off to bring back Diomedes' horses; he had stopped en route at Pherae, where king Admetus received him. It was a warm and hospitable welcome, and the king begged him to spend a few days in his company. But Heracles had other matters to attend to. His duty was to leave for Thrace and carry out the labour Eurystheus had ordered, not linger on at Pherae enjoying himself.

However, he did promise that he would seek him out when all his labours were accomplished, and then they could eat and drink and make merry to their hearts' content.

Now Heracles remembered the promise he had given to Admetus, and decided to make his way to Pherae to enjoy a little pleasant and relaxing company after so many hair-raising adventures.

Life had always been good to Admetus, especially since the day some years before when he had accomplished an incredible feat with Apollo's help. Harnessing a lion and a wild boar to his chariot he had driven them in triumph to neighbouring Iolcus where he won the lovely princess Alcestis as a prize.

Admetus and Alcestis had lived happily ever since and were now the loving parents of two children. Their happiness was so great that many people said that there was no family to compare with them in all the world.

Then a fearful blow came to shatter the tranquil bliss of this adoring couple. And it fell just when the unsuspecting Heracles decided to visit Pherae.

Admetus had taken to his sick-bed, gravely ill, for the heartless Fates had decreed that his life should be short, and now his hour of death had come.

Alcestis was wracked by sobs of hopeless grief. There was nothing she could do to save her beloved. When she saw her children crying it tore her heart still more. Inconsolable herself, she did her best to comfort them.

"Pray to the gods for his delivery, my darlings," she wept, "and they will not let your dear father be taken from us."

She added her prayers to theirs. Admetus' mother and father also prayed, and throughout the city of Pherae services were held for the king's recovery.

Finally, the gods were moved. The sorrowing Apollo, who felt a special love for Admetus, searched desperately for a way to save him. But it was very difficult, for his imminent death was written by the Fates; and these heartless goddesses, alas, were not to be moved by supplication or turned from their purpose by threats. Till now, they had never changed the lot of any mortal, so was it likely they would do it for Admetus?

But Apollo found the way. He made the Fates so drunk he was able to persuade them to rewrite Admetus' destiny. Yet even in their cups they were so harsh and unrelenting that they would not grant Admetus his life without something in exchange. And the new destiny they decreed for him was this:

"The king of Pherae will be saved if one of his close relatives willingly accepts to die in his place."

A troubled murmur spread through the palace when the court learned the news. Though the terms were harsh, Admetus must be saved, for Pherae had never known such a good and worthy king. But which of his relatives would consent to give up life in exchange for his salvation? A sacrifice like this was not an easy one to make. Little by little the voices fell silent and a deadly hush now reigned. One thought was uppermost in each person's mind and all eyes turned on Admetus' father and mother. Everyone knew how much they both loved their son. And then they were so old, and the little life that was left to them so full of pain and cares that death would come as a welcome relief. With bated breath, they all waited to see which of the two would offer to make the great and noble sacrifice.

But at this critical hour, neither Admetus' father nor his mother could find the courage. Even their

..."I will die for Admetus!"
the lovely Alcestis cried ...

parental love was not strong enough to overcome their fear of death. Their horrified imagination was filled with visions of the foul kingdom of the shades and so great was their terror that instead of lifting up their heads they bent them; instead of saying, "we will die for Admetus" they remained silent; instead of choosing a glorious death they preferred to be held in scorn by all who looked on them, although they both had one foot in the grave.

And then what withered old age could not do, hopeful youth both could and did.

"I will die for Admetus!" the lovely Alcestis cried. There was a stunned silence as she went on, "All-powerful Fates! You who hold men's fortunes in your hands! I thank you for changing the destiny of my beloved. Now accept my life and save his. Since it is written that we must part, send me to the pitiless god of death, and not my husband. And as for you, dear Admetus, try to understand that it will be a thousand times better for me in the underworld knowing that you live than to be here on the fair earth while you are groaning in the depths of Hades."

Alcestis' offer was met by an anguished cry from

Admetus.

"No! No!" he shouted. "Take your words back quickly. Say you made a terrible mistake; say the children can't be left without a mother. I, too, would prefer the depths of Hades a thousand times to life on earth without you."

But Alcestis had not made her brave and selfless offer with any thought of taking it back, and beg her as he might Admetus was unable to make his wife alter her decision. Instead, she ordered her serving girls to prepare her bed and bring the clothes in which the dead are laid. She calmly prepared herself, and before lying down went to the altar of Hestia where the eternal, sacred fire of the family burned.

"Hestia!" she cried, "goddess of our house and of our happy days, see what great misfortune has fallen on us now! You have always stood by us, and now we need you as never before! Keep a loving watch over those I leave behind me, and above all, I beg you, guard our children, who are tiny and defenceless. Keep them in good health; guide and illuminate their minds till they grow up and when the time comes for them to be married, give them,

dear goddess, the joy of knowing true love. But if
that love is destined only to fill their hearts with pain,
like mine, then let them never know its joys."

Only with great effort could Alcestis utter these
last words. She no longer had the strength to stand.
She went to lie down on the bed and her condition
grew rapidly worse – but equally rapidly, Admetus
was restored to health.

Feeling her end draw near, Alcestis murmured in
a failing voice:

"Farewell, Admetus! My darling children, I leave
you now!"

"Alcestis! Alcestis, dear one!" Admetus cried,
and, cured now, he jumped to his feet and ran to his
wife's bedside, believing he might help her. But it
was too late. His beloved Alcestis was already dead.

Admetus knelt at her side, torn by uncontrollable
sobs. The whole palace was sunk in grief, and soon
the whole of Pherae.

Amid an outpouring of public grief such as the
world had never seen before, the fairest of women
and the finest mother upon earth was laid to rest.

After the burial, Admetus returned to the palace

a shattered man. He locked himself inside his room and wept inconsolably. But before long the door was opened by two of his men who announced that Heracles, son of Amphitryon, had come to visit him.

"Heracles!" murmured Admetus, as if talking to himself. "Heracles has come to my palace as I once begged him. Yet what a tragic hour to choose! He came for pleasure and good company, when all I have to offer him is my pain and grief. But no!" he cried, "we shall not make the mighty hero sad! Tell him nothing of our great misfortune; and close the doors of the women's chambers in case he hears their cries of mourning. Give him a royal welcome. Place food and drink before him and keep him pleasant company. I cannot show my face before him in my present state, but I will try to see him later."

Everything was done as Admetus had commanded, and Heracles ate and drank, told funny stories and laughed; but eventually he realized he was the only one enjoying himself and that all around him had long and gloomy faces. He began to wonder what was happening and did not know what to think.

A short time later, Admetus appeared. He showed

no joy or warmth on seeing the hero. While Heracles gave him the friendliest of embraces, Admetus turned his head aside and then drew back with drooping shoulders, and not a word of greeting, leaving Heracles both puzzled and worried.

Then a woman came in bearing wine. Her face was covered with a veil.

"What has happened to you all?" the hero asked. "Why do you hide your faces from me and not speak?" And with these words he put out his hand and lifted the veil from the woman's face.

Then he saw her moist and reddened eyes, and her cheeks still wet with tears.

"Tell me this instant! What has happened?" cried Heracles, putting on a fierce and terrible look.

The woman was frightened into speaking.

"How can we seem happy, stranger, when not an hour ago we buried the finest woman who ever lived upon this earth?"

"Alcestis?" Heracles asked, horror-stricken.

"Alcestis," said the woman, bursting into heart-broken sobs.

Then they revealed the whole sad story, and with

each word Heracles' surprise and outrage grew.

"Where is her grave?" he demanded impatiently.

"There," said the woman, pointing through the window to the spot.

The hero stormed out of the room, ran to the grave and bent down to lift the slab which covered it. An unheard-of idea had come into his head.

"What do you want here?" a hoarse and savage voice boomed out from behind him.

Turning round, the hero beheld Charon.

"I want you!" said Heracles, and threw himself upon the creature of the underworld. No mortal had ever dared to cross his path before. This one must be given a hard lesson, one that all mankind would remember and tremble at! He must wrest his soul from him and take it to the dark kingdom of Hades to be tortured for all eternity. But when they came to grips, the hero's strength surprised Charon even more than his boldness. Their struggle was so violent that the earth shook beneath their feet. Heracles seemed the stronger of the two, but Charon tried to blow his deadly breath into his face. The hero realized the danger and forced his head downwards. When Charon did it a second and a third time, Heracles caught him by the neck and pressed so hard that his death-giving breath was cut off completely. He could have squeezed the life out of him had not Charon been immortal. But even so he could not endure a vice-like grip like this. Writhing with pain, his eardrums bursting in his desperate need for breath, he was obliged to admit defeat, and in a choking voice which could scarcely be heard, he gasped:

"Tell me what you want from me, and I shall do it."

Then Heracles relaxed his hold, and leaning down until their faces were nearly touching he shouted fiercely:

"I want Alcestis back alive!"

Charon had never heard such an outrageous demand before, but he was so afraid of the hero he did not dare refuse him. And so he lifted the stone slab covering the grave, took Alcestis by the hand and she, miraculously, rose straightway to her feet.

"Take her," said Charon with a shamefaced look. "She is alive again, only she will not speak for three days." And with these words he disappeared.

Then Heracles covered Alcestis' face with her

..."Look, Admetus!" cried Heracles in a commanding
voice. "Look who I have brought you!"...

veil, and taking her by the hand led her back to the palace.

There he found Admetus, sitting with his head buried in his hands.

"It is time to cast your grief aside, Admetus," the hero told him. "Behold the woman I have brought you." And so saying, he lifted the veil which covered Alcestis' face.

But Admetus did not even glance up to see who the woman was.

"You must be mad, Heracles," he replied, "if you think that I will ever take another wife. How do you think I could put my children, Alcestis' children, into the hands of another when I have lost the finest woman who ever walked upon this earth?"

"Look, Admetus!" cried Heracles in a commanding voice. "Look who I have brought you!"

Unwillingly, Admetus raised his head.

"Oh, gods!" he cried. "What vision do I see before me? Let it not fade at once!"

"It is no vision, Admetus, but the living Alcestis," Heracles replied. "I fought with Charon and defeated him. I can hardly believe it, but I wrested her from him, and here she is! A wife and mother once again. Only be patient for three days, until she speaks again, and then you may celebrate her return. But as for me, I beg you, let me leave now. I came here to feast and make merry, but I no longer wish to do so, for I have already found such happiness that nothing could increase it. Farewell, and may you always be happy." And with these words the hero turned and left.

Overwhelmed with the unexpected joy which now flooded his soul, Admetus could not find a single word of thanks. At last he murmured:

"Farewell, mighty Heracles," but the hero was already far away.

Heracles competes for Iole

Heracles' first thought now was to make for Tiryns but on the way a variety of hopes and plans passed through his mind. Whatever harsh trials he had faced in life, however he had suffered, the knowledge that he had finally overcome all obstacles filled him with satisfaction. Yet he needed something else besides.

His weary soul cried out for a little loving care and tenderness to soften the rough passage of his life.

When the hero reached Chalcis, he learned that king Eurytus of Oechalia had a daughter as lovely as Aphrodite and as wise as Athena and he decided to make straight for this kingdom, which was in Euboea, and seek her hand in marriage. The love of Admetus and Alcestis had made a deep impression on him.

But "men propose and the gods dispose" as the saying has it; and with an enemy as deadly as Hera, it would not be easy for Heracles to follow the path in life he wished.

And so it was that as soon as the hero had worked out his term of service under Eurystheus, the goddess began casting about for a way to subject him once more to the will of some unworthy ruler. Yet since her efforts to destroy him had done nothing but win Heracles ever greater glory, Hera now hit on a better plan.

"If I force Heracles to kill an innocent man," she mused, "the gods will come down harshly on him in their rage. And then, perhaps, I will find the chance to humiliate him so utterly that all the glory he has won till now will be forgotten. He is going to Oechalia now, and this may give me the opportunity I seek. Eurytus is a cunning fellow, and I must make good use of him to achieve my aims."

Eurytus, king of Oechalia, had four sons and a single daughter, the beautiful Iole. But since his wife had died he did not wish to let Iole take a husband, preferring to have her around to take care of him in his old age. However, he did not admit this to anyone, so when Heracles appeared before him he said:

"I shall give you Iole if you can outshoot me in an archery competition: me, or any one of my four sons."

These were the terms that Eurytus always laid down when someone asked his daughter's hand in marriage. And he had his reason: he was sure there were no better bowmen than himself and his sons in all the world. Sure enough, though the finest archers in Greece competed for Iole, all were beaten. It could hardly have been otherwise, for Eurytus had been taught to shoot by Apollo himself, whose arrows never missed their mark.

Heracles took up the challenge and Eurytus was delighted, for he wished to boast that he had outshot this mighty hero, too. But what a mortifying shock he got! For Heracles defeated Eurytus and all his four sons, too.

The king of Oechalia was appalled by the result, for he had no intention whatsoever of letting his daughter marry. Furious at his defeat, he began to hurl insults at the hero.

"Get out of here at once!" he cried. "You and your magic arrows that never miss their mark! Did you think that I would ever give my daughter to the bondsman of Eurystheus?"

"You will pay dearly for your insulting words!" Heracles retorted, "and for breaking your promise to me. I will not forget you, Eurytus – I swear it by almighty Zeus!" And with these words the hero turned angrily on his heel and left.

Iphitus

Eurytus' shameful conduct was approved by all his sons but one, Iphitus.

"It is not right!" he shouted. "We gave our word and did not keep it! We lost the contest and will not admit it. And on top of everything, we insult the man we wronged. And then we call ourselves men! Well, why not heroes, since we are so shameless? Shameless you may be, but I am not. We must give Iole to Heracles, since he beat us fairly, and there is not a worthier man on earth. There is another reason we must give her, too: we do not have the right to let her stay unmarried."

"Be careful what you say, Iphitus!" his father shouted. "Iole shall never have a husband, and get that into your heads, the pair of you! You know full well who gives the orders here, so hold your tongue or you'll live to regret it."

Shortly after this, one of Hermes' sons, a crafty fellow named Autolycus, stole a herd of cattle from Eurytus. Using the magic powers he had, he changed the colour of the beasts so they would not be recognized, then took them to Tiryns, where he sold them to Heracles as if they were his own. Not guessing who the real thief was, Eurytus began to shout that Heracles had stolen them.

"It's obvious," Eurytus cried. "He did it for revenge! He threatened us as much when he was leaving. Of course, he didn't have the courage to come and take them in broad daylight with his sword, but crept up in the night and did his dirty work!"

"Heracles a thief? Impossible!" Iphitus shouted back. "Instead of making wild accusations, why don't we go and find the one who took our cattle, get them back, and give him the punishment he deserves?"

"I don't need your advice!" Eurytus said in fury. "We know who the thief is, and I don't care about the cattle. It's enough for me to know what kind of brother-in-law you would have had us take: a dirty, rotten thief!"

"And I shall prove that Heracles is innocent!" his son maintained. "I will go and search for the cattle alone, and find the real thief."

And without waiting another instant he began the search, following the hoof-marks of the animals, which were visible in the earth. These eventually led him into the Peloponnese, to a stable outside Tiryns. On asking whose it was, he received an answer which dismayed him. The stable belonged to Heracles!

"But this is not possible!" Iphitus exclaimed. "Heracles cannot have stolen the cattle. I shall ask to see him, and I am sure he will help me find the thief."

And that is just what he did. Going to the hero, he told him everything that had happened, why he had followed the animals' tracks, and how they had brought him to Tiryns.

Heracles was none too pleased.

"I got these cattle from Autolycus," he said, "I bought them from him only yesterday. But if you want to be absolutely sure …"

"It is not you that I suspect, gods be my witnesses!" Iphitus interrupted. "I just want you to help me find the thief."

"To find the thief, you must first find the cattle," Heracles replied. "Let's go up to the castle. It gives a view over the whole plain and you will be able to see if your own beasts are grazing there as well."

They went up to the castle, stood on the edge of the ramparts and Iphitus carefully scanned the fields below. In fact, the cattle were right under his nose, but he could not recognize them because Autolycus had changed their colour.

"I can't see a single one," he admitted. "The hoof-prints must have confused me."

This was the moment Hera had been waiting for. She immediately clouded the hero's mind with insane rage. The blood rose to his head and his eyes glared madly. No longer his own self, he cried out in a frenzy:

"The hoofprints didn't fool you! You came here with a purpose, because you thought I was a thief. Now take the punishment that's coming to you!"

And with a violent push he heaved Iphitus from the ramparts.

This act threw the gods into consternation. On mere suspicion, and without examining the facts, Heracles had murdered a true friend. And not only that, but he had killed Iphitus the coward's way, without giving him a chance to defend himself. It seemed to the gods that he had committed the foulest crime imaginable, for none could know that all this was really Hera's doing.

In punishment, Zeus himself inflicted a painful illness upon Heracles. It tortured the hero for so long, without any sign of passing, that Heracles decided to go to Delphi and ask what he must do to have his suffering relieved.

The oracle replied that the killer of an innocent man was not entitled to an answer, especially when he had murdered him in such an unmanly way.

Heracles was insulted by Pythia's words. Tormented by his illness, and longing to be cured, he grew so angry that he seized the tripod on which Pythia sat when she uttered the oracle's replies.

Just at that moment Apollo appeared, ruler of the oracle of Delphi.

"What are you doing there, Heracles?" he cried in a stern voice.

"I am taking the tripod to set up an oracle elsewhere, since yours will not give me an answer!"

Immediately, Apollo seized the other end of the tripod and shouted:

"Put the tripod down, Heracles, before I take it from you by force!"

"Take it if you can!" the hero snarled, giving the tripod a great heave and with that a bitter struggle began.

Sick as he was, and though he wrestled with a god, Heracles fought with such fury that Apollo could not defeat him. But neither could the hero defeat Apollo, and so the struggle dragged on for hours without result. At last, however, Zeus saw what was happening and hurled a thunderbolt between the two to part them. Heracles was thrown one way by the blast, Apollo another, and the tripod a third.

Then Zeus told Apollo he could have the tripod, but that he must also order Pythia to give Heracles the answer he had sought.

Pythia gave the hero this reply:

"Listen, son of Alcmene. The illness you are suffering is a punishment. It was sent by mighty Zeus because you murdered Iphitus without cause. For the sickness to pass from you and your crime to be forgiven by the gods, you must be sold into slavery for two years and the money from your sale be taken by Eurytus in compensation for the son you murdered."

*... Zeus saw what was happening and hurled a
thunderbolt between the two to part them ...*

Heracles serves Omphale

Thus Heracles was obliged to give up his freedom once again. Hermes, god of commerce, undertook to sell him. But before he could do so, the goddess Hera hastened to inform him that she had found a willing buyer in Omphale, queen of Lydia, and it was to her that he went. The renowned hero became the slave of a vain and worthless woman.

Omphale was filled with self-importance to have Alcmene's son as her slave. Not that she wanted him to perform any great labours, but merely to have the hero there and humble him, to make her feel she was his better. What a fool Omphale was! Hera was smugly certain that Heracles would be so humiliated and ridiculed that from now on no one would speak of him with respect, but only with contempt.

Determined to belittle him, Omphale spoke to Heracles as if he were her humblest slave, giving the hero the most menial and unfitting tasks that she could think of. She made him sweep the floors, wash clothes and cook, spin wool and, in a word, do all the jobs reserved for female slaves.

But, strangely enough, the great hero did not seem at all put out at being given such lowly and unaccustomed tasks to do.

"I killed an innocent man," he said, "and I must pay. If I show patience and carry out these menial jobs as best I can, perhaps the soul of Iphitus will forgive me."

And so, however mean the work he was given, and however unused to it he was, Heracles tried to do it well – not for Omphale, of course, but for Iphitus.

Omphale was puzzled by the zeal and willingness which Heracles showed in carrying out even the "humblest" tasks. She racked her brain to find new ways of making him look small, but was galled to see he never took her orders in that spirit. Perhaps she had not learned that no honest job demeans a man. Perhaps she did not know that to become a proper man and a true hero great deeds and shining achievements are not enough, that lowlier tasks are needed, too; however small and insignificant they seem, they must be carried out correctly and with care, for in them is reflected the soul of every man, as well as every hero. But how could Omphale be expected to know such things when even the goddess Hera did not know them and thought that she could degrade the mighty hero thus?

However, the two years that Heracles served Omphale were not taken up entirely with household drudgery; great labours came his way as well, and more than once he faced dangers and hardships.

For example, he killed the ghastly giant Lityerses, who quenched his thirst with the blood of unwary travellers, and tossed his huge body into the foaming waters of the river Maeander. On another occasion, after a fearful struggle, he slew the monstrous serpent of the river Sagaris, which had been tearing men and animals to pieces. A third feat was to face and kill Syleus, a Lydian bandit who forced passersby to tend his vineyard and then murdered them.

The Cercopes

Once, however, an adventure of a very different kind befell him.

It was a hot summer's day, and Heracles had set out early for the neighbouring city of Ephesus, where he had some business to attend to. But the road was long and weary, and at the height of noon he lay down under a shady tree to rest. Soon his eyes closed and he fell asleep. As he lay there, he was spotted by two dwarves. These were the Cercopes, known everywhere for their thieving ways but also for their amusing tricks. They roamed from town to town, their reputation growing as they went, for their great success lay in the fact that after every theft or swindle they pulled off they always managed with their jokes and funny antics to get away scot-free.

Now when the two Cercopes saw Heracles asleep, they decided to steal his weapons. First they took his shield and, carrying it one on each side, hid it behind a bush. Next they stole his bow and arrows and after that they tried to carry off his club, but soon gave up when they found they could not lift it. Stealing the sword was a more difficult matter, for it was tied around the hero's waist, but nevertheless the two little men decided to make the attempt. As they were pulling it out, the hero woke up. The two dwarves were terrified; however, not only did they hide their fear but immediately began doing such funny jumps and somersaults you might have thought they were performing in a carnival. But Heracles knew they had been trying to steal his sword and that their amusing antics were only a cunning trick to distract his attention from what they had been doing. When he looked down and saw his shield and bow were missing, the hero grew red with anger. Although he spotted them almost immediately, behind the bush, he decided to punish the two dwarves. His first thought was to beat them, but he held himself in check. After all, they were such tiny creatures! One blow each and he would kill them. In the meantime, turning head over heels and cracking jokes continuously, the two Cercopes were trying to make good their escape. This crafty manoeuvre did not go unnoticed. A few swift steps and Heracles had caught them.

"So that's what you're up to, eh?" he cried. "Now you'll see!" And grabbing the little men he tied their feet to each end of a pole, hoisted it on his shoulder and took the two dwarves, dangling upside-down, off to Ephesus to be tried.

But the Cercopes were such masters of the art

*... and he took the two dwarves, dangling upside-
down, off to Ephesus to be tried ...*

of making people laugh that, trussed up as they were, they managed to perform such antics and pull such funny faces that Heracles enjoyed his walk to Ephesus thoroughly – so thoroughly that in the end he felt quite sympathetic towards the pair, and set them free. Released at last, the two Cercopes turned a few somersaults more, then made off fast before he changed his mind.

So, thanks to their winning ways, these crafty thieves escaped once more; but not for very long. Heracles may have forgiven them, but his father Zeus was furious at what they had tried to do to his son, and he punished the pair by turning them into stones. And indeed, not far from Ephesus, there is a rock which seems to have the figures of two dwarves upon it. These are the Cercopes, they say, and no more thefts or cunning tricks or jokes for them!

In the end, Heracles served out his time as bondsman to Omphale. By his hard work, reliability and patience he had washed the stain of Iphitus' murder from his soul, and he set off back to Greece a free man once again.

The struggle with Achelous for Deianeira

On his way home he remembered Meleager, who had begged him to save his sister when he descended into Hades to fetch Cerberus.

"Perhaps," he thought, "I have gone through all this suffering because I forgot my promise to Meleager, neglected Deianeira and preferred to compete for Iole, daughter of Eurytus."

And so he decided to go to Calydon, in Aetolia, where king Oeneus reigned, and to ask for the hand of his daughter Deianeira.

When Heracles arrived in Calydon he found a host of fine young men from every part of Greece – and all had come for the same purpose. Asking around, he discovered that Deianeira's father, Oeneus, had decided that a wrestling contest would be held and that his daughter would be given to the victor. However, among the would-be bridegrooms there was a fearsome and unbeatable opponent, the river-god Achelous. This being had the power, when he was wrestling, to turn himself into a snake, and then a bull, and then a man again. But most often he appeared in a form which was a combination of the three, with a gigantic snaky body, the arms of a man and a human head crowned with two bull's horns. And as he was a river-god, foaming waters flowed from his thick beard. Deianeira could not even bear to look on him, and she would have preferred to die rather than become his wife.

All the other suitors stared at him in terror, and one by one they withdrew from the contest. How could they wrestle a monster such as this!

But Heracles decided to compete.

Achelous laughed scornfully.

"I am stronger than you, and a better man by far," he boasted. "No one has ever beaten me, and I am feared by gods, let alone by men. Why, at Dodona they even make sacrifices in my name. I am the father of every river in Greece, and not a wandering slave!"

"Better by far? At what?" came Heracles' retort. "Only at hurling insults and defeating your opponents with your looks – if you call that victory; but I shall vanquish you with my bare hands." And with these words he hurled himself upon him.

Achelous was taken by surprise. Such daring and such strength had never challenged him before. He fought like a lion, but he soon realized that he could not hold his own against the hero. So then he resorted to his other arts. Changing himself into a snake, he began to slither out of Heracles' arms. Immediately he found himself caught by the neck in a grip of steel. Fearing that he might be strangled, Achelous next transformed himself into a bull, but then the hero caught him by the horns, lifted him into the air and threw him backwards to the ground. Such strength did the hero put into his throw that one horn was left in his hand, and Achelous, crashing to the ground, let out a terrifying roar of pain.

"Now what do you have to say?" cried Heracles in a terrible voice.

"Give me my horn back and take Deianeira for yourself," was Achelous' shamefaced reply.

And so the son of Zeus was able to marry the daughter of Oeneus and after a little while he took his wife and went to set up home in Trachis, where king Ceyx ruled. Ceyx was a friend of Heracles and his wife Alcyone would be able to keep Deianeira

company when the hero was away from home. But on the way they had to cross over the river Evenus. There they found the centaur Nessus who, for a small sum, would carry travellers to the other side. So Heracles lifted Deianeira onto Nessus' back while he himself swam across.

But when Nessus reached the further bank, instead of setting Deianeira down he galloped off, determined to steal the hero's lovely wife.

Then Heracles drew his bow, and for all the speed
of Nessus' flight, he loosed an arrow steeped in the
Lernaean Hydra's venom, which reached its target
and sank into the centaur's body. Nevertheless, before he died Nessus thought of a way of revenging
himself on Heracles, and so he said to Deianeira, "I
have done you a great wrong, and to make up for it
I wish to be of use to you. Take a jar and collect the
blood which is flowing from my wound. Should you

ever fear that your husband may leave you for another woman, then choose a moonlit night, sprinkle a garment with this blood and give it to Heracles to wear. Your husband will return to you immediately, for my blood has this magic power."

Deianeira did as Nessus said and hid the blood without suspecting anything, not even knowing that in that blood was mixed the hideous venom of the Hydra.

Heracles and Deianeira lived happily together for a number of years and she bore him four children, the eldest of whom was named Hyllus.

Heracles reduces Troy

But naturally enough, the hero did not spend all his time at home, for he could not live without performing great deeds and acts of valour.

And so it was that a short time after his marriage he decided to lead an expedition against Troy to punish Laomedon, the king who had kept his word neither to the gods Apollo and Poseidon, nor to Heracles himself, when he saved his daughter Hesione from a frightful death.

Gathering a band of brave young men from Trachis and other parts of Greece, Heracles set sail for Troy with eighteen ships. Among the willing volunteers was Telamon, of course, for the hero from Salamis had not forgotten Hesione for a single moment.

Heracles surrounded Troy and quickly prepared for the attack. As soon as the order to advance was given, Telamon lunged forward. Nothing could hold him back. Breaching a section of the walls, he was the first man into the city. But when he saw Heracles coming up behind him, he was afraid that the hero might be insulted that he had not let him enter first. So, bending to the ground, he began to pile up stones.

"What are you doing there, Telamon?" Heracles enquired.

"Building an altar to Heracles the Victor," was Telamon's quick answer.

Now, either because he was taken in by this, or because he admired Telamon's resourcefulness, the hero was pleased by this reply. Remarking only that there was no time to be lost now, he drew the young man to his feet and, followed by the rest of their brave band, led the charge on Laomedon's palace. Battle was joined at once, and the efforts of Heracles and his companions were soon crowned with victory. Laomedon was killed and many prisoners were taken. Among them were Hesione and her brother Podarces.

Heracles handed the lovely Hesione over to Telamon, whose joy was indescribable.

But Hesione stood there with a heavy heart.

"I grieve for the evil which has fallen on our city, and for my father's death," she said. "I know he was to blame, and so I bow my head to those who once saved my life. But my sorrow will only be lightened if you set my brother free."

"If there is anyone who should become a slave, it's he!" roared Heracles. "He was lucky to escape with his life!"

But Telamon cast a beseeching look at the great hero, begging him to do the favour Hesione asked.

Heracles realized what he wanted and turned his words, but not his voice, which he purposely kept stern.

"So we shall not set him free, unless," he added, "you buy him back." Now Hesione had no means of purchasing her brother's freedom. It was an anxious moment for her, till suddenly an idea came into her head and she offered timidly, "I can give you my veil."

"Splendid!" cried Heracles, and not only did he set Podarces free but he made him king of Troy as well, renaming him Priam, meaning 'he who has been paid for'.

At last, they all boarded their ships and set sail for Greece.

But on the voyage, Hera found another chance to do the hero harm. Sending the god of sleep to Zeus to sink him in deep slumber, she enlisted the help of the north wind and raised such mountainous waves upon the sea that Heracles and his companions were in danger of their lives. Finally the ships were driven to the island of Cos. There they found a harbour and sailed in to escape from the raging seas, but even in this refuge great peril lay in wait for them. The inhabitants of the island believed that they were pirates and began throwing rocks at them from the shore, and Heracles himself was struck by a flying stone. The heroes were obliged to go ashore and fight back. The islanders were soon defeated and when they saw who their victors were, felt so ashamed of the welcome they had given them that they presented them rich gifts to turn aside their wrath.

In the meantime, Zeus had woken up. He opened his eyes to see a wounded Heracles fighting with blood gushing from his wound. Angry and worried, he came down from the heavens in person, carried his son from the battlefield and took him to the ships, where the wound was bound and the bleeding held in check.

The great lord of gods and men had often been angry, but never as furious as this. He realized that it was all the work of Hera; and in his rage he caught her, bound her arms with massive chains of gold and hung her from the clouds, between the heavens and the earth. And to make her suffering more painful still he tied two great iron anvils to her feet, stretching her legs till she was in unbearable agony. Torn by hideous pangs of pain, the great goddess cried out piteously for help. But who dared set her free when mighty Zeus warned all the gods that if they did he would fling them from Olympus to the earth below, where they would breathe their last, immortal though they were? Yet however painful Hera's sufferings may have been, they were light besides the torment that racked mighty Zeus when he thought of all the dangers his son had been through. For he loved Heracles more than all the gods together.

The hero may have been in deadly peril, but that did not stop him from setting out at once on another adventure which was more dangerous still.

The battle with the Giants

The children of Mother Earth, the invincible Giants, had declared a savage and relentless war upon the gods. And now the goddess Athena, who had often helped Heracles both openly and in secret, came in her turn, to seek the hero's aid. Her face was pale with fear, for the Giants were terrifying creatures. Their faces were hideous to behold and their hair and beards a wild, sprouting mass. Most frightening of all, their legs were thick, writhing snakes. Their size and strength were enough to make the boldest quail. They could pluck whole mountains from the earth and hurl them at their enemies. The Giants were not only stronger than the gods but outnumbered them ten to one. As if that were not enough, Mother Earth had once given them a magic potion so they could not be harmed by the strength or weapons of the gods. Confident of their awesome power, the Giants had now decided to cast the gods down from Olympus and make themselves the new rulers of the earth. It would be a black day if these hideous beings achieved their aim. The world would lose its beauty, and pain and suffering become mankind's only companions.

The war that now burst out was terrible. Not since the battle of the Titans had earth seen such a conflict, and never had the gods found themselves in such danger. At one point the Giants pursued the gods to Olympus itself, piled great rocks like mountains one upon the other and would have stormed the palaces of the immortals, had not Zeus then loosed a rain of thunderbolts which crashed upon them like the ending of the world and forced them to withdraw. Now the war was raging in Chalcidice, the homeland of the Giants.

But if the Giants were invulnerable to the weapons of the gods they were not proof against mortal arms. All that was needed was a hero brave enough to face them, though finding such a man was no easy task. Heracles was the only hope and that is why Athena had now come to the great hero. Perhaps his strength and daring, and the arrows tipped with the Lernaean Hydra's poison could save the day for the Olympians.

Heracles ran to join them in the fight.

Way up in the north, on the headland of Chalcidice, a terrible struggle was in progress. Gods and Giants were locked in a combat so fierce that the whole earth shook to its foundations. Zeus' thunderbolts crashed down in ceaseless volleys and the skies lit up and echoed without pause. The gods were fighting like lions, but against hopeless odds. It seemed that nothing could even scratch the Giants, and they were on the point of casting the immortals into Tartarus. At this very moment the fearsome son of Zeus entered the battle, causing instant consternation.

One, two, three of Heracles' arrows winged
through the air and three massive forms dropped
dead. They were the first Giants to die in the battle. The fourth shot hit huge Alcyoneus in the chest
but it had no effect on him. Athena ran to warn the
hero that the Giant was immortal while his feet were
planted on Pallene, the land where he was born.
With a sudden lunge, Heracles caught him up in his
brawny arms and carried him off to another place,

where the terrible creature immediately dropped dead.

Another Giant, Porphyrion, was now pursuing Hera. The undying hatred which the goddess felt for Heracles did not make the hero hesitate to save her, and with another poisoned arrow he shot Porphyrion dead. The astonished Hera cast a shamefaced glance at Zeus' son. Such nobility of spirit was beyond her comprehension. She asked herself what her fate would have been – indeed, the fate of all the gods – if any of her plans to destroy Alcmene's son had ever met with success. But there was little time now for such thoughts, for combat was still raging.

Now seven Giants were hunting Aphrodite. Heracles awaited his moment and killed them one by one. The gods fought with new courage, for the Giants' powers were fading. From the moment Heracles began to shoot them down, they became vulnerable to the immortals' weapons, too. Caught on Athena's long spear, the Giant Pallas died. Hephaestus dealt a hideous burn to Clytious with a red-hot iron. Dionysus killed Eurytus with his staff, and four more were killed by Hermes, Artemis and the Fates. But Ares beat a hasty retreat when faced with Ephialtes. Apollo, though, was able to wound the awesome Giant, and Heracles rushed to finish him off.

The Giants saw victory turning to defeat. They realized that the cause of this was Heracles, and ten of them suddenly launched themselves upon him. But the hero did not lose his nerve. One after the other he shot his arrows into them. Had but one shot gone astray they would have had the time to kill him. But each one found its mark and all ten Giants fell lifeless to the ground. Now the conflict was drawing to its close. Heracles' arrows and Zeus' thunderbolts were felling the last remnants of the enemy. Two Giants only were left, and they took to their heels with the gods close behind them. Poseidon caught up with Polybutes near Cos, tore a mountain from the island and smashed it down upon his head. And thus the neighbouring isle of Nisyros was born. Enceladus, the most dreaded of all the Giants, was hunted by Athena over land and sea till finally she pinned him down by heaving the whole of Sicily upon his body. Even then, Enceladus did not die. Buried deep beneath the island he writhes and shudders, often causing disastrous earthquakes right across the world.

And that is how the Battle with the Giants was said to be. It is the high point of the hero's achievements in the eyes of men, even to the point of their imagining him victorious over the Giants, and saviour of the gods.

Nessus' revenge

With the Battle of the Giants we have come to
Heracles' last feat. There only remains to be told of
his expedition against Oechalia to punish Eurytus: an
expedition crowned with victory but which brought
disaster on the hero. An expedition which brought
Heracles' life on earth to an end but which caused
him to be raised to Olympus and made immortal.

Heracles had never forgotten Eurytus and his
sons. He could never forgive them for breaking their
word and refusing him Iole, or for submitting him to
such insult and contempt.

But why should the hero still have been haunted
by this old story? After all, he now had Deianeira
for his wife, and what did it matter if they had not
given him Iole as they'd promised?

Yet Heracles had sworn Eurytus would be punished. A long time had passed since then, and he
could no longer let the matter rest. Besides, backed
up by his sons and his strong army, Eurytus continued to hold the hero in contempt, and even boasted
that the cowardly Heracles was afraid of him. He

had gone as far as claim that Alcmene's son had given solemn vows of revenge and then broken them, openly calling him an oath-breaker and forgetting how dishonourably he and his sons had once behaved towards him.

Thus Heracles was obliged to mount the expedition against them.

A host of brave young men came to join his ranks and soon a whole army was assembled. The expedition set out, Oechalia was overthrown and Eurytus was killed with all his sons. But that is not the important part of this story.

From the prisoners which had been taken, Heracles selected two or three men and a larger number of women and sent them home to Deianeira in the charge of one of his men, Lichas.

Deianeira immediately noticed that among them was a young woman of stunning beauty who held herself nobly and was dressed like a princess.

She first asked Lichas who the woman was, but he pretended not to know, so next she asked a prisoner and learned that this was Iole, daughter of Eurytus.

Bitter jealousy welled up in Deianeira's heart.

She was terribly afraid that Heracles might take Iole for his wife, for she was younger and more beautiful.

Whether Deianeira was right or wrong in her suspicions, we are never told. Nor do any of the myths reveal whether Heracles wished to take Iole for his wife. The hero was so popular that even if he had been at fault, no one would have wished to reveal it.

But jealousy is a bad counsellor, and it prevented Deianeira from thinking the matter over sensibly and coolly. Instead, her mind flew straight to the idea of using the centaur Nessus' blood to hold onto Heracles' affection.

Going to a chest, she drew out a wonderful robe which she had woven with her own hands, went out into the courtyard and there, by moonlight, dipped it in the blood of Nessus, not knowing, poor woman, that this blood had been tainted with the Hydra's poison, the most venomous in the world. Her task completed, she put the robe inside a box and called for Lichas.

"Go to Heracles at once," she instructed him. "In this box is a robe which I wove for him with my own hands. Tell him that I wish him to wear it when he sacrifices to almighty Zeus."

And Lichas took the box containing the poisoned robe and disappeared full speed into the night to carry it to Heracles.

In the morning, Deianeira saw something which nearly drove her mad with horror. In the courtyard, where she had sprinkled the robe with the blood of Nessus, the flagstones were discoloured. Now, as the sun came up and began to warm the stones, the blood began to boil and bubble with green foam. Soon the stone slabs had been eaten through by the terrible poison. And then she realized what she should have known from the start: that Nessus had wanted to kill Heracles in revenge, not help her keep a hold on him.

Beside herself, Deianeira called for Hyllus, their eldest son.

"Run to Oechalia!" she gasped. "Do not stop a single instant on the way. You must prevent your father from putting on the robe which I have sent him. It is poisoned!"

"What are you saying, mother?" the boy asked in surprise. "How could you do such a thing?"

"Don't waste time with questions! Run to save your father from a hideous death!"

Hyllus ran like the wind. He ran as if all the furies were behind him. But he was too late. Heracles had prepared himself for the sacrifice early in the morning, eager to wear the gift his wife had sent him. But when the sun rose shortly afterwards and its golden rays fell upon the robe, the poisoned blood with which it had been sprinkled began to grow warm.

At that moment a voice was heard!

"Take off the robe! It is poisoned!"

It was Hyllus, and as soon as he had gasped out the words he fell to the ground, exhausted by his desperate run.

As he did so, the hero's body was suddenly wrapped in hideous agony. He tried to tear the robe off but in vain. The cloth had stuck to his skin, and in his efforts to pluck it from him he pulled the flesh from his body. Horrible pains were rending him asunder. The hero who had never let a cry of pain escape him in his life, however much he'd suffered, now let out such cries that they reached the heavens themselves. And among them were heavy curses on

Deianeira for the evil she had done him.

"Take me away from here," he groaned. "This place is choking me. Bear me to Trachis so Deianeira may see her handiwork."

So they placed Heracles on a ship and brought him back to Trachis.

Hyllus ran to find his mother, and as soon as he caught sight of her he shouted:

"You have killed the finest man that ever graced this earth, the greatest hero the world has ever known!"

Deianeira let out a tormented shriek and ran back to the house, crying out loud, tears streaming down her face. Then the cries were suddenly cut short. Hyllus ran inside and a terrible sight met his eyes. His mother lay dead in a pool of blood.

Hyllus sped back to his father.

"Mother has killed herself!" he told him.

But Heracles was writhing in such agony that he may not even have heard him.

"Take me to the summit of Mount Oeta," he groaned. "I wish to die there, closer to the gods."

When they had carried him to the mountain top,

he ordered them to gather wood for a funeral pyre and to place him on it.

Then Heracles told Hyllus to look after his young brothers and sister and, when he came to manhood, to take Iole as his bride. Last of all he ordered:

"Light the fire now!"

They all looked at each other. Who could light the fire? Who could burn the mighty hero alive, though they knew that to die in its flames was a lesser torment than the agonies he was suffering now?

"Light the fire, I say!" Heracles shouted once again. But still no one made a move.

"Hyllus, light the fire!"

But the boy could not do it.

"Fire! Fire! Does nobody pity me enough to light the fire?"

The hero's terrible suffering tore at their heartstrings. But none of them would make the first move.

And then a famous archer named Philoctetes appeared. He pitied the great hero, and when Heracles promised him his arrows dipped in the Lernaean Hydra's venom, he agreed to put a torch to the pyre.

Heracles ascends to Olympus

But before its flames had even touched the hero, the heavens were rent by thunderclaps and the whole scene lit up with Zeus' lightning bolts. A chariot drawn by four winged horses swooped down from the sky. In it stood Athena and Hermes. At the same time nymphs came running from the woods with jars of water and put out the fire. Athena and Hermes took Heracles by the hands and the hero stood up, instantly cured. They placed him in the chariot and at once the horses spread their splendid wings and soared off towards Olympus.

There Heracles was received by all the gods. Zeus and Hera stepped down from their thrones to welcome him. It was a moment that touched the hearts of all who saw it. Heracles and Hera were reconciled at last, and she called her daughter Hebe to offer nectar to the new god. Then, taking the girl's soft white hand, she placed it in the hero's broad palm. All the gods gave them their blessing, and soon a splendid wedding was arranged. Heracles married Hebe in the shining palaces of the gods and lived happily on Olympus ever more.

But although the mighty hero had departed from the earth, he was not forgotten by mankind. Everywhere sacrifices were offered up and temples built in his name, and in every city athletic contests, the Heracleia, were held regularly in his honour. But above all, men loved to tell tales of his astonishing achievements and the countless hardships of his troubled life. They had more to say of Heracles than any other hero – or any god, for that matter. For he was loved so much in his time that his name has remained immortal, though thousands of years have rolled by since.

WHO IS THE TRUE HERACLES? This question will
arise in any reader's mind if he studies the wide range of
texts which provided the sources for this book. For the
myths relating to Heracles suffered more alterations and
additions with the passage of time than any other chapter
of Greek mythology. The harm was not done by additions
more or less in the original spirit, but by others, with an
ulterior motive; foreign to the true figure of the hero, they
distort his character and are the expression – if they express
anything at all – of an era bearing no relation to the heroic
age in which the myths were first set. Thus, in researching
the sources, one finds the most contradictory claims made
about the son of Alcmene, and careful selection is needed
in deciding which of them is truly representative of him
and which not.

In making the choice for this book, all additions were
rejected which wilfully distort the original myths; nevertheless, some useful conclusions can be drawn from their
study, and for that reason alone they are mentioned here.

The additions fall into three categories.

The first, and oldest, is that which links the hero's name
with numerous women, making him the father of a vast

number of children. Granted, presenting a hero in this light is not unusual in Greek mythology, but in Heracles' case such additions are in direct conflict with the life and deeds of a hero seeking atonement for his sins and whose actions are repeatedly characterized by self-denial. They damage the hero's moral character, it is true, and cloud our understanding of his true aims, but on the other hand – and this is important – they show that Heracles was such a widely admired figure that many wished to claim him as their father. For this was indeed the case, and it is worth noting that all the extra children later attributed to him were male. What it amounted to was the exploitation of a great name by numerous rulers – and naturally, the greater the exploitation, the greater the name had to be. Curious though it may seem, if we wish to assess the popularity of a god or a hero in Greek mythology we should count, among other things, the number of children he is said to have fathered on mankind; and in this respect Heracles scores higher than Zeus himself. Nor should it be forgotten that while man's love for the gods was rooted in fear, his love for Heracles stemmed from admiration and was thus of even greater worth. In fact, Heracles was reputedly the father of something like ninety children. After the hero's death there was said to have been – and probably was – a long period of wars named "the return of the Heraclids", the Heraclids being the children or descendants of Heracles.

Around this time, many kings in Greece claimed that they were sons or direct descendants of Heracles, and these were later imitated by certain kings of Asia Minor. In time, it was even said that the colonisers of Sardinia were descended from him, and furthermore that various mythical leaders such as Scythes, Galatis and Celtus, from whom far distant peoples took their names were sons of his, too. All of which goes to show how far the fame of the hero eventually spread.

But where the Heracles myths have suffered most is not in this first category of additions, but in the other two: those which depict the hero as a pervert and those which seek to ridicule and belittle him – for in time that, too, became his lot.

The former variations are not, I think, worth dwelling on; particularly since certain rulers with unnatural proclivities claimed – obviously in an attempt to justify themselves – that the great hero had indulged in the same vices. Indeed, such practices were attributed to the gods themselves and again it is a case, however undesirable, of the exploitation of a great name. It must be stressed, however, that all these distortions occurred in much later times – further proof that they form no part of genuine Greek mythology.

Even more foreign to the spirit of true mythology are those additions made with the intention of demeaning Heracles. Such ulterior motives moved the Athenians, for example, who wanted to establish their own hero, Theseus, as a greater figure than Heracles. Thus Heracles became the target for humiliation once again, many centuries after the period in which he was supposed to have lived. Various insulting incidents were tagged on to his life-story telling, for example, how Omphale dressed him up in woman's clothing, and painting an overall picture of a man who wasted his life tilting at windmills and was anything but famous for his intelligence. And since, in time, Athens became the cultural focus for the whole of Greece, this image of the hero still prejudices those who neglect to consider that these were additions with an ulterior motive and, too, of a much later date. Granted, Greek mythology almost never depicts a god or a hero as entirely faultless, which is in itself proof that the myths have their origin in actual events. The same holds true for Heracles, but without detracting from the fact that he was a just and noble figure: this shines through all his troubled life and deeds. He was sharp-witted, too – the most ancient sources cite his wisdom. He had not yet entered adolescence when he defended himself in court and astounded his judges by the clarity of his reasoning. While still a youth he armed the Thebans in a manner which showed the inventiveness and powers of decision of an inspired leader, and went on to conduct the war against Orchomenus with all the skill of a seasoned general. And Heracles proceeded to put the same seal of resourcefulness and wise reasoning on all his labours. In brief, Heracles was quick-minded, just and great-hearted, and again it becomes clear that had he not possessed these qualities in such abundance no need would ever have been felt to diminish his stature. The rulers of Athens would never have wished to belittle Heracles had the people of the city not loved him even more than their own hero, Theseus.

Thus, all three kinds of addition, while seeming on the surface to lower the hero's standing, finally bear witness to a single fact: that Heracles enjoyed greater popularity than any other god or mortal. Students of the mythical period should begin to ask themselves seriously why this hounded and exploited hero should have won such high esteem, and at last seek out the true Heracles. But if he is to be found, I believe that theories such as his being the personification of the sun or a figure from non-Greek myth should be abandoned, and proper consideration given to the possibility that perhaps the Heracles of myth was the glorified image of a hero who really lived in those distant years and achieved fame by humbling the "great king of Mycenae" to the dust, or by defeating and punishing Erginus of Orchomenus, Augeias of Elis, Diomedes of Thrace, Laomedon of Troy, Eurytus of Oechalia and other kings still, without ever becoming a king himself.

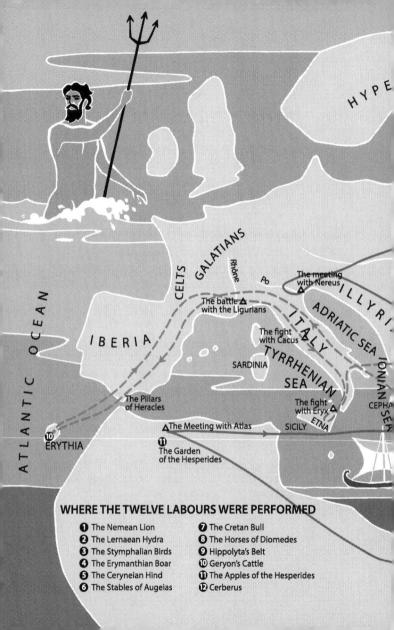

WHERE THE TWELVE LABOURS WERE PERFORMED

1 The Nemean Lion
2 The Lernaean Hydra
3 The Stymphalian Birds
4 The Erymanthian Boar
5 The Ceryneian Hind
6 The Stables of Augeias
7 The Cretan Bull
8 The Horses of Diomedes
9 Hippolyta's Belt
10 Geryon's Cattle
11 The Apples of the Hesperides
12 Cerberus

HERACLES' TWO
GREATEST JOURNEYS
--- - --- The tenth labour
——— The eleventh labour

AEANS

SCYTHIANS

CAUCASUS

BLACK SEA

THRACE

...crus (Danube)

△ The meeting
with Prometheus
COLCHIS

Strymon

❽ Abdera
CHALCI-
DICE   THASOS

Bosporus

● Heracleia
The battle
with the Bebrycians

AMAZONS

❾ Themiscyra

...US
...e fight
...th Cycnus
● Pherae

Hellespont

MYSIA

● Troy

PHRYGIA

EUBOIA
● Thebes
● Athens

Ephesus
●

LYDIA

...ni

❶ ● Mycenae
❸ ● Argos

● CILICIA

PONNESE
● Sparta

PAROS

COS

SYRIA

❶❷

CYPRUS

● Sidon

CRETE ❼ ● Cnossus

PHOENICIA

The fight △
with Antaeus

The Temple
of Zeus Ammon
●

EGYPT

Nile

GREEK MYTHOLOGY SERIES

* * *

An index of names for all volumes in this series
can be found in volume 4, 'Theseus, Perseus'
and on our web site: **www.sigmapublications.com**.

The site also includes **mythological maps**
and extensive extracts from all our books.